FRANCESCO PETRARCH

ON RELIGIOUS LEISURE
(DE OTIO RELIGIOSO)

❧

FRANCESCO PETRARCH

ON RELIGIOUS LEISURE
(DE OTIO RELIGIOSO)

Edited & Translated by
Susan S. Schearer

Introduction by
Ronald G. Witt

ITALICA PRESS
NEW YORK
2002

ITALICA PRESS, INC.
595 MAIN STREET
NEW YORK, NY 10044

Library of Congress Cataloging-in-Publication Data

Petrarch, Francesco, 1304-1374.
[De otio religioso. English]
On religious leisure / Francesco Petrarch ; edited & translated by
Susan S. Schearer ; introduction by Ronald G. Witt.
    p. cm.
    ISBN 0-934977-11-9 (pbk.: alk. paper)
    1. Christian life—Early works to 1800. I. Schearer, Susan S., 1945-
II. Title.

BV4500.P4813 2002
248.4'82—dc21

                                                              2002004701

Printed in the United States of America
5 4 3 2 1

Cover Art: The Cloister of Fontenay Abbey, France. Photo © Italica Press.

FOR A COMPLETE LIST OF OUR TITLES IN HISTORICAL STUDIES
VISIT OUR WEB SITE AT: HTTP://WWW.ITALICAPRESS.COM

CONTENTS

❧ ❧ ❧

V

*To Ron and Hartley
and the laurel tree
in Petrarch's garden
at Fontaine de Vaucluse*

PREFACE

My acquaintance with Petrarch's *De otio religioso* began in a seminar sponsored for American teachers by the National Endowment for the Humanities and held in Avignon, France, in July of 1992. Since my high-school days the study of ancient Latin literature has been my primary intellectual interest; and as a high-school teacher in the Winchester, Virginia, public schools for thirty years, I have had the goal to instill in my own students the same passion I have felt for the literary and historical works that the Western world has for centuries regarded as "classics."

The seminar, led by Prof. Ronald Witt of Duke University, was devoted to a study of the major writings of the great fourteenth-century humanist, Francesco Petrarch. Although Italian by birth, Petrarch had lived most of the first fifty years of his life in southern France in the area of Avignon, and most of his works were either completed or conceived there. The seminar met principally in Avignon, but occasionally we convened in Petrarch's garden at his residence below the cliffs of Fontaine de Vaucluse about forty-five minutes by car from the city. The tranquillity and natural beauty of that garden remain with me and inspire me as they must have affected Petrarch.

Professor Witt had asked each of the fifteen members of the seminar to prepare a short report on other works of Petrarch not included in the common reading in order to amplify our understanding of Petrarch's humanism. Because I was a Latin teacher, he asked me (along with Paul Sullivan of Austin, Texas) to report on the *De otio,* the only major work of Petrarch that had not received an English translation. It was my first contact with neo-Latin literature, and once I began reading the Latin, I lost myself in its words. Although I cannot say that I found in them a purpose for my life, as I read, I discovered a meaningful sense of solitude in the hustle and bustle of the world near the end of the twentieth century. I resolved by the close of the seminar to make this text, which seemed to me to be as valuable as the rest, available to other readers of English.

For eight years, while maintaining an intense teaching schedule, I spent the short summers and other odd hours working on the text. The division into two books is Petrarch's, but the division into chapters is my own. In this entire task I have been aided by Professor Witt, whose knowledge of the fourteenth century and of late Latin helped me to understand better the context in which Petrarch was writing.

In this undertaking I have incurred a series of obligations besides that to Prof. Witt. A number of his students at Duke University have read my full English text over the last few years and have helped to improve it by their comments. Paul Graziano, a graduate student in Renaissance history at Duke, made a significant contribution to the translation by thoroughly comparing the Latin text with my English version. I also owe a tremendous debt both to the National Endowment for the Humanities, which made possible the contact between a university professor and a high-school teacher, out of which this translation grew, and to the University of Virginia's Center for the Liberal Arts, which underwrote my 1993 summer's work on this project. Finally, I want to acknowledge the support of my husband Hartley Schearer, whose own love of Latin literature gave him an understanding of the task I had undertaken and whose devotion maintained my resolve over so many years.

Susan S. Schearer
June 2002

INTRODUCTION
BY RONALD G. WITT

At some point in January or early February of 1347, Petrarch briefly visited the remote Carthusian monastery of Montrieux, where, four years before, his beloved brother, Gherardo, had pledged himself to live in perpetuity as a *renditus*, one who took the same vows as a monk but who was not cloistered.[1] In the day and a night he spent at Montrieux, Petrarch spoke privately with Gherardo, had lively discussions with other residents, and attended religious services celebrated by the brothers with "angelic singing."[2] Unwilling to disturb the rigid discipline of the monastery longer, he reluctantly departed the next morning accompanied by the prior and the brothers to the limits of their property and he imagined them continuing to watch him until he disappeared from view. [3-4]

Returning to the Vaucluse, still "mindful of that whole blessed sweetness which I drank in with you," and troubled that in the course of the hasty visit he had not been able to say many things that he would like to have said, he decided "to express in writing what I was not able to do in person." [4] The body of the work that was to become the *De otio religioso* was composed sometime during Lent or between February 11 and March 29 of that year. Not untypically, however, Petrarch continued to add to the text as late as 1356, and the finished treatise was probably not dispatched to Gherardo until 1357.[3]

In the decade between his visit in 1347 and the completion of the manuscript, Petrarch saw his brother only once more, probably in April 1353, for a final farewell on the eve of what was his own definitive departure from Provence for Italy. With the exception of his brother, he encountered only new faces in the monastery.[4] In the summer of 1348, in the first onslaught of the Black Death in Provence, abandoned by their prior, who later died in his homeland of the disease which he fled, the entire population of the monastery, except for Gherardo, had perished. There is no indication of the second visit having had any effect on the writing of the still incomplete text.

The two brothers had been close since childhood, and Petrarch had been deeply involved in his brother's decision to leave the world for the monastery. A few years younger than Petrarch, Gherardo had probably followed his brother in Convenevole da Prato's grammar school at Carpentras, and when their father decided to send Francesco to Bologna to study law in 1321, Gherardo, apparently destined for the same profession, accompanied him along with a tutor.[5] The death of their father ser Petracco in 1326, however, altered the course of their lives. Having inherited his wealth, the two young men returned to Avignon to enjoy the fashionable society of the city. It was a life given over to banquets and dances.[6] Because they felt constant pressure to dress and act like young men of the world, the mature Petrarch referred to these countless rounds of entertainments as "toilsome sweetness."[7] Ankles and leg tendons suffered from the tight stylish shoes; the tight bands, which they wound around their heads to keep their painfully constructed coiffure in place overnight, made their foreheads red and wrinkled in the morning. They lost hours in deliberating about the clothing they would wear when going out.[8] Both sought to establish a reputation as poets by writing vernacular love lyrics, Petrarch to Laura and Gherardo to his *bella donna.*[9]

While both brothers eagerly sought pleasure in the best circles of Avignonese society, Petrarch's participation was from the beginning limited by his devotion to his studies. After 1330, when it was discovered that the money from their father's estate, administered by trustees, had disappeared in questionable circumstances, Petrarch was forced to become a client of the Avignon branch of the powerful Colonna family of Rome, and his free time was even further restricted. In Gherardo's case, the change in circumstances does not seem to have interfered significantly with his pursuit of amusement. "Weak and uncertain," uninterested in learning, something of a spendthrift, Gherardo became a source of "fear and worry" for Francesco.[10] Despite its elegance, this was a violent society and Gherardo's escapades could easily have ended with his death in a duel.[11]

A sudden change came over Gherardo in the early 1340s. Since the autumn of 1337 he and his brother had been living in the valley of the Vaucluse, a day's trip outside Avignon.[12] If Petrarch had chosen his new residence in order to lead a more reflective life, there is no reason to think that Gherardo joined him in this and that the younger brother had given up participating in the social life of the nearby papal city. The death of his *bella donna* about 1340, however, radically affected him.[13] Writing to his brother from Padua in December 1348, Petrarch, referring to the recent death of Laura and to the earlier death of Gherardo's beloved, praised God for having saved both men from their own passions:

> That so great a [love] not oppress us, You have provided in Your mercy that the objects of our delight be taken away and in so doing Your right hand has plucked from the earth our hopes when they had barely taken root. You have called them to You in their youthful years by death, which, I hope, was as useful to them as it was necessary for us.[14]

Nonetheless, the loss was painful:

> How many sighs, how many laments, how many tears did we pour out to the winds, and like madmen who revile their physician, we rejected Your hand when it tried to apply the best of all salves to our wounds!

Petrarch's Sonnet 91, "The beautiful lady whom you so much loved," written in 1340 or early in 1341, seems to have been an attempt to console Gherardo and to interpret his lady's death in a positive light.

> Since you are lightened of your greatest burden, you will be able to put down the others easily, rising like a pilgrim who carries little.[15]

Gherardo was to understand this recommendation in his own way. Petrarch left Provence for Italy in February 1341, and when he returned a year later in February 1342, he found Gherardo considerably changed. The subject of joining a monastery now became a major focus of their conversations.[16] Nonetheless, when Gherardo finally did decide, he did so "suddenly."[17] As late as March 13, 1343, when Clement VI acceded to Gherardo's petition for an appointment as secretary in the papal penitentiary, he had not yet made up his mind. It may have been only then that Gherardo, forced by the papal action to decide, swore to take vows in the Grotto of Sainte Baume, very near the monastery of Montrieux, where Mary Magdalene was believed to have lived as a penitent. By Easter, April 13, a month after the papal announcement, Gherardo was probably already a member of the monastery's family.[18]

Gherardo's entry into the monastery compelled Petrarch to examine more intensely his own singular way of life. Over the next decade he frequently returned to the contrast between his brother's choice of the straight and secure route to heaven and his own contradictory efforts to move in the same direction. His account of the ascent of Mt. Ventoux with his brother (*Fam.* 4.1) is his most famous representation of the contrast. Written between 1345 and 1350, but claiming to be an account of the brothers' ascent of the highest mountain in Provence in 1336, the narrative depicts Gherardo, prepared to accept the difficulties of a direct climb to the top, reaching the summit long before Petrarch finally arrived after losing considerable time in seeking an easier way. Similarly, the first poem in Petrarch's *Bucolics*, apparently composed in 1347, about the time of the *De otio*, recounts the discussion between Silvius (Petrarch) and Monicus (Gherardo), the former a singer of Vergil and Homer, the latter of David. Although Silvius promises to turn soon to sacred studies, he must first devote himself to finishing his *Africa*.[19]

Doubtless, the rigorous monastic discipline of Montrieux held a strong attraction for Petrarch in that it offered him a proven prescription for harmonizing the conflicts in his soul and increasing his chances for eternal life. But at the same time, Petrarch was aware that he could not surrender to the restraints that monastic routine would impose on his freedom to explore his own subjectivity. He knew as well that his passion for expanding his knowledge of ancient pagan and Christian texts, a knowledge which was necessary to guiding this self-exploration, could never be satisfied within the walls of any monastery.

The *De vita solitaria*, composed in large part during Lent in 1346, revealed the complexity of Petrarch's view of his own style of life.[20] On the one hand, he was perfectly aware of its uniqueness in his own time and of its debt to antiquity: he was a cleric, living in retirement, without clerical duties, unattached to a court, devoting his days to the study of literature, much of it pagan, and to writing learned works and vernacular love poetry. On the other, he anxiously needed to legitimate his manner of life by envisioning the *otium* he practiced in the Vaucluse as continuous with the *otium* first identified with the monastic life by Augustine.

In Roman antiquity the term *otium* had had the general meaning of being free from action and from the preoccupations that are the companions of activity, that is, equivalent to a quiet life (*quies*), freedom from care (*securitas*) or tranquility (*tranquillitas*).[21] By Seneca's time (d. 65 C.E.), however, a more specific meaning of *otium* developed as signifying the way of life leading to spiritual enrichment. For Seneca the word could not be understood simply as rest or leisure: "They are not unoccupied whose pleasures are made a busy occupation." Rather, "of all men they alone are at leisure who take time for philosophy, for they alone really live." Wise men in leisure, moreover, have "accomplished greater things than if they had led armies, held public office, and made laws...."[22]

From Augustine on, a line of Christian thinkers espoused the monastic life as the true embodiment of *otium* because, detached from the cares of the world, it provided the conditions necessary for the attainment of the Christian spiritual life.[23] The Benedictines, Cistercians, and Carthusians of the eleventh and twelfth century were particularly given to discussing the benefits of *otium* or *quies*. Pietro Damiani (d. 1072) praised "salvific *otium*" and the "unimpeded rest of spiritual *otium*," while Peter the Venerable (d. 1156) spoke of "the happy *otium* of the unemployed already participating in eternal beatitude."[24]

The remarks of the Carthusians are particularly relevant in this regard. "Here [in the monastery]," writes St. Bruno (d. 1101), founder of the order, "one strives to acquire that eye whose glance ravishes the spouse with love [Cant. 4:9] and in whose purity God is seen. Here one devotes oneself to an active leisure and reponds in tranquil action."[25] Guignes (d. 1136), fifth prior of the Grande-Chartreuse, stressed as well the active character of monastic *otium*: "it [the solitary life] remains in repose while never being idle. It so multiplies its works that it is more frequently short of time than lacking varied things to do."[26] Study is encouraged but especially of "authoritative and religious books" in which more attention is paid to "the depth of meaning than to the froth of words."[27]

In contrast, the Victorine contemporaries of Guignes and the Dominicans and Franciscans in the next century were deeply ambivalent in their use of *otium*. They shared this attitude with forerunners of Augustine, Tertullian and Lactantius, and with Augustine's contemporary, Jerome. Whereas for these Church Fathers *otium* was frequently a synonym for "the quiet life" (*quies*) and "peace" (*pax*), it could also be taken to mean "idleness" (*otiositas*).[28] Similarly, thirteenth-century Franciscan novices were advised to avoid *otium*, and St. Thomas, while recognizing that the word might mean simply "free time," also saw it in the negative sense as idleness: "*otium* is relieved by meditating on the sacred Scripture and divine praises."[29] By the fourteenth century the negative sense of *otium* prevailed, and in the next century even a major Carthusian writer like Dionysius (d. 1471) employed it in this way.

If Petrarch's use of *otium* in a positive sense was in effect a rehabilitation of a disappearing usage, he almost certainly was unaware of it. Rather, in the *De vita solitaria*, as has been suggested, he tried to extend its meaning so as to justify his own way of life in the Vaucluse. His task was facilitated, first of all, by the work's omission of any direct comparison between the monastic life and his own; and secondly, by the welter of heterogeneous examples adduced in its latter half to illustrate the solitary life. Examples of Old Testament and New Testament figures, and of popes, monks, and friars are followed by others from pagan antiquity, such as Homer, Anaxagoras, and Cicero, and a certain Brahman, Calandus by name. As a result, the definition of *otium* dissolved into such incoherence that Petrarch could easily make of it what he wanted.

At one level, the *De otio* was a contribution to the ancient debate between the relative virtues of city and country life, but at another, the dichotomy had soteriological implications. In other words, Petrarch seems to have felt compelled to set pagan *otium*, which envisioned the life of retirement as a means of reaching moral perfection, within a Christian context where it became the way of salvation. He did this by making very clear that his prime concern in withdrawing from the affairs of men was to save his soul from shipwreck. At the same time that he realized the good he could have done by helping others to find their way to God, he was so beset by his own moral conflicts that he was forced to renounce the active life and to think only of saving himself.[30] He was careful to say, however, that by "solitude" he did not mean to imply living by oneself. The presence of a like-minded companion did not disturb solitude, but rather enriched it.[31]

While conceding that solitude did not create of itself a tranquil spirit — "it is conducive to preserving and strengthening" inner peace already acquired — Petrarch insisted that it did contribute "something" to its acquisition.[32] In his case, at least, life in solitude was the best way of cultivating a spiritual disposition. At the same time, he would not recommend it to all men because for many, especially those "who have no acquaintance with literature," solitude would be "more grievous than death."[33]

In his most extended statement on the spiritual state produced by his literary *otium*, Petrarch did his best to relate it to his salvific concerns. By means of the study of literature he aimed to reach the contemplative heights from which to view the world and oneself as passing away in time and, thereby to realize that "this life is but the shadow of life," to desire not fleeting things but those that endure, to submit to circumstances, always mindful of the promise of immortality, and to:

"range in imagination through all ages and all lands; move about at will and converse with all the glorious men of the past," and sometimes to rise, with thoughts that are lifted above yourself, to the ethereal region, to meditate on what goes on there and by meditation to inflame your desire, and in turn to encourage yourself and [bring near your heart already alight, as it were, the torches of burning words] — these are not the least important fruits of the solitary life....[34]

But, he hastened to add, the solitary life afforded "more obvious pleasures":

to devote [yourself] to reading and writing, alternately finding employment and relief in each, to read what our forerunners have written and to write what later generations may wish to read, to pay to posterity the debt which we cannot pay to the dead for the gift of their writings, and yet [in so far as we are able] not remain altogether ungrateful to the dead but to make their names [known if they are unknown], to restore them if they have been forgotten, to dig them out if they have been buried in the ruins of time and to hand them down to our grandchildren as objects of veneration, to carry them in the heart and as something sweet in the mouth, and finally, by cherishing, remembering, and celebrating their fame in every way, to pay them the homage that is due to their genius even though it is not commensurate with their greatness.[35]

If designed to demonstrate the role of study undertaken in *otium* as preparation for Christian contemplation, these passages revealed, nonetheless, the inherent tension between the cultivation of disdain for the things of this world and Petrarch's desire to celebrate the authors of antiquity with himself as their champion. The incongruity of his efforts became even more obvious in the closing sentences of the book where he felt called upon, in the name of Christian piety, to divide what he had earlier presented as a continuum.

...the original source of eloquence [the writings of the ancient pagan writers] allures us by clear brilliance of style but it is without the true light of doctrine. It soothes the ear but it does not give repose to the mind nor lead it to that highest and securest enjoyment, that peace of intellect to which...there is no approach save through the humility of Christ.[36]

Had Petrarch been completely convinced that pagan learning was in fact a dead end soteriologically, as he suggested here, he might easily have explained why, even in his retirement, he continued to be beleaguered by passions:

> As for my present solitude — why should I boast of what I do not possess? It is not that solitary life for which I yearn, although outwardly it bears a near resemblance, being equally withdrawn from the human crowd but not equally emancipated from human passions. Oh, could I but behold that ineffable sweetness which is felt by blessed souls at the remembrance of the struggles they have passed through and the prospect of the joys to come....[37]

The overall tone of the *De vita solitaria*, regardless of the work's contradictions, however, constituted a positive endorsement of his style of life. At one point he conceded that his love of solitude derived from his love of books, from his aversion to the crowd, and from his fear of gossip about his life, suggesting that at least initially worries about the other life had been secondary.[38] There can be no question, however, that by the time he wrote the *De vita solitaria*, despite his failure as yet to acquire the spiritual gifts he sought, he believed that his own best hope for obtaining them lay in a life of *otium* in which prayer and study were intermingled.

Compared with the *De vita solitaria*, the *De otio religioso* has aroused little interest on the part of scholars. Both in content and form it is among Petrarch's least humanistic writings. An unrelieved tirade against the world, drawing widely on the reservoir of arguments collected from pagan writings, Scripture, and the Church Fathers, Petrarch's treatise appears at first reading to fit easily into a well-established genre of writing on human misery, dedicated to urging Christians to abandon the world for the monastery and, for those already there, to persevere in their endeavor. True to the form, his approach was monolithic, and the area of ambiguity that often provided fertile ground in Petrarch's other writings for the expression of new insights was very limited.

Stylistically, Petrarch's Latin is less classicizing than in most of his other work.[39] Apparently designed to be read aloud in a refectory, the sentence structure is essentially paratactic with almost no clausal subordination. In contrast with most of the author's other Latin writings, an individual accustomed to hearing Latin sermons would have been able to follow his thought at least in outline. Directed to a monastic audience, the *De otio* manifests no specific links with lay spirituality.

From the outset, however, Petrarch reoriented the *De miseria hominis* tradition: he was not primarily interested in recruiting new monks or in encouraging those at Montrieux to remain faithful to their vows: "long ago you made a deeply-rooted habit of conduct for yourself." [5] Rather, he was writing for himself. He made no secret of the spiritual gulf that separated him, "a sinful man who is tired, ignorant, and overwhelmed with care," from his audience, "our Lord's bees, a well-born race." [4] As with so many of Petrarch's other works, he was writing down his thoughts so that "I may hear myself speaking and heed what I say." [5] Also distinctive of Petrarch's approach were (1) its tendency to dramatize arguments by presenting them in the form of an interchange between his own voice and that of the soul's tempters and (2) its preoccupation with contrasting pagan and Christian cultures. These innovative adaptations of a medieval genre at the very least manifest humanistic tendencies on the part of the author.

Petrarch's originality becomes even more obvious when *De otio* is compared with a work in the same genre written by the leading humanist in the generation after Petrarch's. The response to a request of a monk who wanted a treatise confirming his decision to take vows, Coluccio Salutati's *De seculo et religione* (c.1381), like the *De otio*, offered an all-embracing condemnation of life in the world and a glorification of withdrawal from it.[40] At points, although nowhere as extensively as in Petrarch's treatise, it contrasted pagan and Christian cultures with a view to affirming the absolute condemnation of the pagans, regardless of the virtues they possessed.

Although in his proemium Salutati confessed his diffidence as a sinful layman in composing a treatise designed to teach the value of the monastic life, once he set to work persuading the monk of the wisdom of his decision, he assumed the role of an advocate for the monastic profession and displayed no personal involvement in the issue. With the exception of a few moments of fresh insight, on the whole the work was much closer than the *De otio* to the traditional genre. It should be said, however, that neither treatise proved to be popular with later humanists.

Within Petrarch's whole corpus of writings, the *De otio* represented his most coherent presentation of the ascetic position that persistently undercut his confidence in the capacity of pagan learning to contribute to the moral reformation intrinsic to the salvific process. It must have increased doubts Petrarch had about his sojourn in the Vaucluse and may well have inspired the direct confrontation of Franciscus with Augustinus in the *Secretum*, whose first draft was completed in the same year.

The opening sections of the *De otio* are dedicated to praising the life of religious leisure. In two authoritative commands: "Take time and see [that I am God," Ps. 45:11] are given, Petrarch declares, "whatever you must do, whatever you must wish and hope for, not only in the transient life, but in the life eternal." [5] In fact, the two commands are but one because the second, "seeing" God, is the result of time. [6-8] All other occupations require fatigue and sometimes incur great danger in the expectation that once the labor is accomplished, rest will follow. But in reality, those who spend their time laboring will continue to do so after death. For the ascetic alone rest produces rest [7]. By rest, Petrarch does not intend "inactivity," but rather "leisure, and that for religious purposes." [14]

As Petrarch describes "leisure," it entails freedom

> from those superfluous tasks which wear out our body and spirit from the carnal desires which defile and weaken our whole person, from the visual lusts which deflect us from the acquisition of knowledge, from the ambitions of this age which ensnare us with their claws and shackles, from useless concerns which inflame our heart with unseen torches, and finally from all sins which torture, oppress, and destroy our unhappy soul. [14]

In this state of leisure, free of passion and even free of the memory of one's past, the soul lies open and offers maximum receptivity to the Divine Word. As he writes succinctly later in the *De otio*:

> blessed with the required free time for that extraordinary contemplation of salvation which alone has been the goal of your struggle, neglecting all other concerns, frugally, soberly, and watchfully take advantage of this great gift of God. [64]

After providing an extensive series of biblical quotations designed to furnish guidance and comfort to Christian souls [15-19], Petrarch launches into the body of the work. He formally divides the treatise into three parts according to the three major enemies of the soul, demons [24-78], the world [81-91], the flesh [94-112], but so interconnected are the workings of these sources of sin that he frequently has difficulty keeping their treatments apart. The remainder of the work is devoted to a comparison of ancient pagan religion with Christianity. [115-48]

Petrarch begins with the "invisible enemies" led by the devil, who, spurred on by jealousy and pride, plots "against no one more than against the servants of Christ." [24] He will never cease wandering "about your

sheep folds like a roaring lion and a famished wolf." [30] Among the
many anxieties that he tries to incite, he especially raises doubts about
the validity of Christ's promises and tries to arouse despair of salvation in
the soul borne down by sin. Petrarch then turns to the world and the
flesh, which distract the soul from the path to salvation by offering alluring but deceptive pleasures. Especially dangerous to Petrarch's mind is
the attraction of the flesh to luxury, the youngest and most seductive of
the seven daughters of the devil. [110]

Although the catalogue of human miseries is largely traditional,
Petrarch's interpretation of the remedy is quite his own. To the devil's
urging that God provide signs to prove Christ's promises, Petrarch insists
that the historical foundation of Christianity proves their validity. To do
this, he devotes large sections of the work to discussing the relationship
between pagan and Christian beliefs and the extent to which pagan thinkers, even the best of them, failed to arrive at Christian truth through
reason. Indeed, Petrarch's treatment of these issues here is the most extensive in his corpus of writings.

"There was never a people," he maintains, "so crude or inhuman that
they did not believe in the existence of God." [33] Wise pagans like Cicero,
moreover, doubted the divinity of the gods whom they worshipped. [115]
He as well as Livy frankly admitted that many of the gods had been mortals, who, subsequent to their deaths, had been exalted to divine status
because of their deeds. [116-17] While Cicero seems at one point to distinguish between certain gods who were always heavenly and others raised to
heaven by their people, it seems likely that he really believed that all the
gods "left earth for the heavens." [123] The pagan practice of euhemerism
would not have been too destructive spiritually had not demons occupied
the statues of the gods. [124] Taking advantage of the worshippers' credulity, these demons had themselves honored as gods. With the coming of
Christ, however, the devils fled their shrines and fell silent. [49 and 124]

Although ignorant of the true import of what they were saying, some
ancient authorities spoke words prophetic of Christian truth. In proving
this, Petrarch gives most play to the prophecies of the Erithrean Sibyl,
who, "even if she was speaking about Augustus Caesar," predicted the
advent of John the Baptist and described the major events in the life of
Christ — all of this before the Trojan war. [40-42] Similarly, although
intending to speak of Augustus, Vergil uttered prophetic words about
the divine mystery of the Incarnation.

In contrast, the prophets of the Old Testament were conscious of the significance of their predictions, and with the Incarnation the prophecies became facts. Yet the Jews refused and continue to refuse to believe in Christ: "depriving themselves of this present joy through ignorance and arrogance, [they] torture themselves with a meaningless hope for the future and a very stupid expectation." [35] As a consequence of their lack of belief, they have been sorely punished: Titus destroyed their city of Jerusalem with immense loss of life, and their people were dispersed throughout the whole world. They were "saved only as a mockery of themselves and as a witness of Him, Jesus Christ, Whom they had crucified." [35]

But if the fate of the Jews is not enough to counter the doubts raised by the devil, we can assault these doubts with the "sharp arrows of an All-powerful God, together with coals of desolation," [67], that is, with the Apostles whose message has now spread throughout the world, and with the wounds of the martyrs, who testified to the faith by their excruciating deaths. [68 and 71] Doubtless, miracles were helpful in converting a pagan population in the early days of the faith, but to require them now, as the demons urge, is to "demand the whole story of the Gospels to be repeated."[75-76] This is superfluous in an age when "God's word has pierced the chests of kings and populations with a wound which causes, not intense pain, but sweet love." [68]

But even acknowledging the truth of Christ's promise of eternal life, Satan endeavors to make us believe that the weight of our sin makes it impossible for us to merit such a reward. He would delude us into forgetting that for God nothing is impossible. For the God who brought about the union of human with divine in the Incarnation, what is not possible? Trapped by the thinking of the natural world, we believe that a cause cannot operate unless the object on which it is to act is prepared for the action.

> Let nothing terrify us: God's power is not limited by any natural boundaries. Not only does it exercise its own power over those objects which are disposed, but it also disposes what has not been prepared. [38]

In this passage as elsewhere throughout the work, Petrarch insists that, when one conceives of God, rationalistic, naturalistic thinking is out of place. This is one of the major criticisms he subsequently levies elsewhere against scholastic philosophy, especially in *On His Own Ignorance and That of Many Others*. Out of place as well is a corollary of this way of thinking, the notion of human justice, which metes out punishment and reward in the measure that one's acts are good or evil.

> When a man decides that God does not wish to have mercy on those who repent and that His mercy is limited to the amount man himself sins, he is ignorant of God or fails to consider His power and mercy. However great the sin of mankind may be, it is certainly finite, but the goodness of God and His power are infinite.... [38]

Sin is not in the senses but in the mind, and a mind fortified with faith that God is omnipotent and all-merciful can resist any temptation, whether of the devil, the world, or the flesh. Left to ourselves in the natural world, we are fragmented by desires and in despair; trusting in the mystery of the Incarnation and our fellowship with Christ, we are confident of the future.

In the concluding pages, Petrarch comes back to himself by confessing that the Scriptures, which he now adores, were earlier in his life an object of ridicule for him. He lays the blame on his teachers, who communicated their attitude to their pupils, and on parents more concerned with the worldly status of their sons than on their spiritual growth. He relates that his first reading of Augustine's *Confessions* in 1333 marked the beginning of an interest in Christian literature, one which over time led him to intensive study first of the Church Fathers' writing and then of Scripture itself.

> Thus, full of awe, with the very illustrious company, I entered the realm of sacred Scriptures, which I had previously scorned, and I found that everything was contrary to what I had thought. A therapeutic need brought me to praise God and to my daily obligation to glorify Him, which I had wrongfully put off. For this reason, I have often been forced to reflect upon David's Psalms, a source from which I have been eager to drink, not that I might became a more learned man, but a better one, if I could, not that I could come out of it a better dialectician, but a less corrupt sinner. [146-47]

He says nothing, however, as to whether or not his reading has changed him. Indeed, the work ends with the same contrast in spiritual states with which it began when he admonishes the monks to "continue in the direction...you have begun" and to "weep for me."[148]

In preparing his edition of *De otio* on which the present translation is based, Rotondi discovered that there were two versions of the text, a shorter version on which all earlier editions had been based, and a longer version best represented by Vatican Library, Urbinate lat. 333.[41] Considering the latter to be the latest version of the text, Rotondi based his edition on the Vatican manuscript after collating it with the same version as it appeared in National Library, Paris, Lat. 6502 and British Library, Harley 6348. We are still lacking a critical edition of the work.

❧   ❧   ❧

NOTES

1. The reconstruction of the events surrounding Gherardo's entry into Montrieux and Petrarch's two visits there is found in Henry Cochin, *Le Frère de Pétrarque et le "Livre du Repos des Religieux"* (Paris: E. Bouillon, 1903) and Arnaldo Foresti, "Quando Gherardo si fece monaco," in his *Aneddoti della vita di Francesco Petrarca: Nuova edizione corretta e ampliata dall'autore*, Studi sul Petrarca 1 (Padua: Antenore, 1977), 108-14; and in the same volume "Un saluto e un sospiro alla Certosa di Montrieux," 194-203. On the status of a *renditus*, see Raymond Boyer, *La Chartreuse de Montrieux aux XIIe et XIIIe siècles*, 2 vols. (Marseille: J. Laffitte, 1980), 1:151-52, 168 n. 26 and 214-15.

2. The English translation of the *De otio* is based on the version of the work found in *Il "De otio religioso" di Francesco Petrarca*, edited by Giuseppe Rotondi, Studi e Testi 195 (Vatican City: Biblioteca Apostolica Vaticana, 1958). Most of the notes are also taken from his edition.

    The citation in the text is found on page 4 of the translation. All page numbers found in brackets in the text of my introduction refer to the translation that follows. The basis for Rotondi's Latin text is discussed below. An excellent Italian translation of the work is found in Petrarch, *Opere latine*, ed. Antonietta Bufano with B. Aracri and C.K. Regiani (Turin: UTET, 1975), 567-809.

3. Cochin, *Le Frère de Pétrarque*, 200-201; and G. Martellotti, "Introduzione," p. xiv, in *De otio religioso*, P.G. Ricci, trans. In *Prose*, G. Martellotti, et al., eds., La letteratura italiana, Storia e testi 7 (Milan & Naples: Riccardo Ricciardi, 1954).

4. Cochin, *Le Frère de Pétrarque*, 74-80.

5. *Fam.* 17.1: *Le familiari*, 4 vols.; vols. 1-3 ed. Vittorio Rossi, vol. 4 ed. Vittorio Rossi and Umberto Bosco; Edizione nazionale di Petrarca, vols. 10-13 (Florence: G.C. Sansoni, 1934-1942), 3:222. In the notes below where *Le familiari* is cited, the book and number of the letter are given first and the volume and page in Rossi's edition follows.

6. *Fam.* 10.3; 2:296.

7. Ibid., 2:289.

8. Ibid., 2:290-91.

9. Ibid., 2:292. The two young men sang "inane little songs filled with false and despicable praises of young girls, in an open confession of foul lust." In Petrarch's *Canzoniere* 91, written in consolation for the death of Gherardo's beloved (see below, n. 13), the poet refers to her only by that name.

10. Cochin, *Le Frère de Pétrarque*, 19, has the references.

11. Ibid., 24.

12. *Fam.* 10.4; 2:303. "Three years ago," Petrarch writes, "while I was visiting France, the heat forced me to go to the fountain of the Sorgue, which, as you know, was where we once had chosen as our permanent residence."

13. On the basis of its ordering in the collection by Petrarch, Foresti, *Aneddoti*, 113, dates the poem of consolation to Gherardo on her death as written in 1340 or 1341.

14. *Fam.* 10.3; 2:292.

15. Robert M. Durling, *Petrarch's Lyric Poems: The "Rime sparse" and Other Lyrics* (Cambridge, MA and London: Harvard University Press, 1976), 195. See above n. 13.

16. *Fam.* 10.4; 2:306.

17. *Fam.* 10.3; 2:290: "But a sudden transformation effected by the hand of God brought you out of the thick shadows of error." See as well Ibid., 16.9; 3:199: Gherardo was "suddenly changed."

18. Foresti, *Aneddoti*, 111. The text of the appointment is published by Carlo Cipolla, "Note petrarcesche desunte dall'Archivio vaticano," in *Memorie della r. Accademia delle Scienze di Torino. Classe di scienze morali, storiche e filologiche*, ser. 2, 59 (1909): 4.2.

19. See Nicholas Mann, "The Making of Petrarch's *Bucolicum carmen*: A Contribution to the History of the Text," *Italia medioevale e umanistica* 20 (1977): 130-32. For the poem with English translation, see Thomas G. Bergin, *Petrarch's "Bucolicum carmen"* (New Haven & London: Yale University Press, 1977), 2-15.

20. Of the *De vita solitaria* only the first book exists in a critical edition: *De vita solitaria. Buch I. Kritische Textausgabe und Ideengeschichtlicher Kommentar*, ed. K.A.E. Enenkel (Leiden & New York: E.J. Brill, 1990). An English translation of the work is found in *The Life of Solitude by Francis Petrarch*, trans. Jacob Zeitlin (Urbana: University of Illinois Press, 1924; reprint, Westport, CT: Hyperion Press, 1978). I will use Zeitlin's translation but I will substitute in brackets my own translation in cases where his does not reflect the text of the critical edition. On the date of the first draft of the work, see *De vita solitaria*, xxi.

21. The following four paragraphs are based on Jean Leclercq, *Otia monastica: Étude sur le vocabulaire de la contemplation au moyen âge*, Studia Anselmiana 51 (Rome, 1963): 27-41; and H.J. Sieben, "'Quies' et 'Otium,'" in *Dictionnaire de spiritualité ascétique et mystique, doctrine et histoire*, vol. 12 (Paris: Beauchesne, 1985), 2746-56.

22. The passages cited are respectively: *De brevitate vitae*, 13.1 and 14.1; and *De otio*, 6.4.

23. Leclercq, *Otia*, 37-40; and "'Quies,'" 2748-49.

24. "'Quies,'" 2751.

25. *Letter*, 1.6: *Ad Radulphum, cognomento viridem, remensem praepositum* in *Lettres des premiers chartreux. I. S. Bruno-Guignes-S. S. Anthelme*, Sources chrètiennes, Sèrie des textes monastiques d'occident 10 (Paris: Editions du Cerf, 1962), 70. Cf. "'Quies,'" 2753.

26. Guignes, *De vita solitaria ad ignotum amicum*, 1.4, in *Lettres des premiers chartreux*, 144.

27. Ibid.

28. "'Quies,'" 2748, 2750 and 2753-54.

29. Ibid., 2753-54.

30. *The Life of Solitude*, 130.

31. Ibid., 164.

32. Ibid., 126-27.

33. Ibid., 131.

34. Ibid., 150. The words in brackets here and in the next citation are my translation based on the critical edition.

35. Ibid., 151.

36. Ibid., 316.

37. Ibid., 142.

38. Ibid., 148.

39. For a brief stylistic analysis of Petrarch's Latin in the work, see my *"In the Footsteps of the Ancients": The Origins of Humanism from Lovato to Bruni* (Leiden & Boston: E.J. Brill, 2000), 272-73.

40. The work was critically edited by Berthold L. Ullman as *Colucii Salutati De seculo et religione ex codicibus manuscriptis primum edidit B.L. Ullman* (Florence: L.S. Olschki, 1957). See my discussion of the work and scholarly comment on the work, *Hercules at the Crossroads: The Life, Works, and Thought of Coluccio Salutati* (Durham, NC: Duke University Press, 1983), 195-208.

41. On the edition, see Giuseppe Rotondi, "Le due redazioni del *De otio* del Petrarca," *Aevum* 9 (1935): 27-77; his "Note al *De otio religioso*," *Studi petrarcheschi* 2 (1949): 153-66; and the introduction to the edition by Guido Martellotti, "Introduzione," v-xv.

FRANCESCO PETRARCH

ON RELIGIOUS LEISURE
(DE OTIO RELIGIOSO)

BOOK I

THE BOOK OF FRANCESCO PETRARCH,
THE POET LAUREATE,
TO HIS BROTHER GHERARDO,
A MOST RELIGIOUS MAN,
BROTHER OF THE CARTHUSIAN ORDER,
ABOUT RELIGIOUS LEISURE,
BEGINS WITH GOOD WISHES

I

O blessed family of Christ, it would have been appropriate while I was with you to say something which my devotion and our common love of God would recommend to your faith. However, as you have seen, my time there was too brief to free my mind burdened with cares. Since all the sweet moments of this life are usually more fleeting than the wind, I arrived (it seemed) at the same time that I left, and so I can use Caesar's saying in a truly different context: "I came, I saw, I conquered."[1] Certainly if "winning" means fulfilling one's wish, the winner is the person who satisfies his wish.

So I have won because I achieved what I wanted: I came into paradise; I saw the angels of God living on earth and in earthly bodies, destined to live in heaven and to come to Christ, for Whom they now do battle, after the present toil of their earthly exile has been completed. Had Christ not known you "before he formed you in the womb,"[2] had He not blessed you and predestined you to be among the number of the chosen, He would in vain have shown you this straight and burdensome path, remote from the pathways of the world.

Lest I hope for anything fully rewarding here on earth, however, the very brevity of my visit with you weakened that wonderful sense of spiritual joy which I gained from our conversations. I scarcely had the chance to look upon your venerable faces. Never was a day shorter, a night faster. While I was contemplating your most holy hermitage and shrine, while I wondered at your devoted silence and angelic singing, while I admired you, all together at times and at times individually, and while (as is natural to humanity) I embraced my beloved brother, my sweetest treasure whom I had entrusted to you, and while I took pleasure in the conversation I had so much wanted with my best and only brother, the whole brief time fled by me without my realizing it.

I had no opportunity to put words together and to collect my thoughts. Your continual indulgence and love (not that common love which you show to all guests in Christ, but a certain singular and fervent love) made me concerned lest my staying longer might perhaps stand in the way of your praises of God and your duties, and these considerations caused me to hasten my departure. Furthermore, my discussions on different subjects with each of you — so many that they could not be long — were pleasant and brief, but always inspired by a blessed and sobering desire for the same objective. They made me forget everything except the words which came forth in turn from the mouth now of this man, now of that one, as if from as many heavenly oracles.

Why should I say more? Thus it happened that I departed, almost in silence, intent and gaping in wonder at everyone and looking around at everything, hearing words on all sides and saying things in bits and pieces. You all accompanied me as far as the limits of your very strict religious order allowed you. Finally you followed my departure as closely as possible with your eyes (I presume on the basis of our mutual affection), your minds, and abundant prayers hoping that I, who had come seeking one brother, had found many.

Now finally having returned to my own solitude and mindful of that whole blessed sweetness which I drank in with you, our Lord's bees, a well-born race, and now, thinking over the experience in private, I find many things of long-term benefit which that all-too-brief stay has given to me. At this point I remember what I overlooked in the rush while I was there. Here now I mean to make good my intention and to express in writing what I was not able to do in person, if only my voice is strong enough, the voice of a sinful man who is tired, ignorant, and overwhelmed with care. In whatever way possible, my fingers will pay the debt of the tongue. I do not know whether it may be any more pleasing, but certainly it will be more long-lasting; for although spoken words, which sometimes may be of heavy substance, may fly away, even light ones, when written, remain with us. So I shall write.

If it is not important to you to hear me write that long ago you made a deeply-rooted habit of conduct for yourself, it is nevertheless important to me to say such things, if it can be done, so that I may hear myself speaking and heed what I say and not be talkative and deaf at the same time, which is a sickness common to preachers. Indeed, I shall control my pen so that my letter to those who are distant may be for me something like a conversation with those who are present, although (to confess the truth) I may be present only in both the nobler and better part of myself.

Where now should I begin, or what should I say first since I am only partly there with you? What else but that saying of David which I wanted to say when I was with you in person: "Take time and see (that I am God)."[3] As you know, that kingly prophet and prophetic king put that exhortation in the forty-fourth psalm. Unless I am mistaken, in these two authoritative words of command [*vacate et videte*], spoken by the spirit of God, albeit through the mouth of a man, are contained the course of your whole life, all your hope, all your motivation, and your final destiny. Whatever you must do, whatever you must wish and hope for, not only in this transient life, but in the life eternal, I pray that you take time and, in so doing, see.

O blessed souls, O guardsmen who are constantly alert, O concerned and devoted servants of Christ, in return for your brief service you earn not just eternal liberty, but also an unstained birth and a filial relationship with Christ. What a reward to be wished for! What a fortunate turn of events! To be a servant for a short time, so that you may rule, not merely for a long time, but forever! For how many years did Jacob serve a man so that he might gain a mortal spouse! "They seemed to be only a few days in comparison to the magnitude of his love,"[4] for thus it has been written. Nor did he earn what he wanted until he served double his period of servitude.

The eternal bliss of an immortal wedding is promised to you who serve God. Serve Him eagerly. He grazed a large and foreign flock among the thickets of humanity. You graze your sheep; that is, each person grazes his own soul in the happy, abundant pastures of Jesus Christ. Serve Him free from care. You do not have a deceitful master such as Laban, whom Jacob endured, who envies your goods and your profits, but One Who may be delighted by your profits and progress, One Who aids you in your need and sustains you in your weakness.[5] Each one of you may truly be able to say about Him, even if you are humble and poor: "My Lord is concerned for me; my Lord rules me, and nothing will be lacking for me; He has set me in His pasture; I have thrown my burden on my Lord, and He Himself will nourish me; I have revealed my path to my Lord; I hope in Him; and He Himself will accomplish it."[6]

So take time and rejoice, you who have earned such a Master by right of His compassion alone. Aristotle says "We do not take time now so that we may have time in the future."[7] You, however, should take time now so that you may have time for eternity. Recognize and appreciate your lot in life, which comparison with other ways of life will manifest. Sailors traverse the seas. They travel on every side of the earth. They wander unceasingly on foreign shores amidst winds and waves and reefs, amidst dangerous straits and all the threats of heaven, with stiff limbs and their hair dripping from icy rain. They pass hellish nights, while many things terrify the wretched men throughout their journey. As Vergil says: "All signs portend impending death for the men."[8]

What sort of miseries and danger do military men not undergo, for whom it is a perpetual game to suffer rains and winds and hail? They spend the night under arms. They lie on the ground. They expose themselves voluntarily to the sword. Falling to the ground face down, they strike the bloody earth with their helmets so that they may not be considered weak and afraid if they act with any hesitation. They receive wounds without feeling them, and they meet death, which is the least of these injuries, but the last one. They are thrown away naked and unburied as prey for wild beasts and sport for birds, and the reward of such ill-treatment is glory and victory over an enemy who is destined to die. Often their tiny reward is less. Is there any wage-earner anywhere more desperate than these soldiers, any man more debased?

What about the labor of farmers? What of the worry of merchants? What of the long nights spent by scholars? What of the sweat of artisans? What of the unspoken fear of those who live in luxury? What about humanity's struggles? What about the zeal and conniving of the ambitious? I ask you, what is the result of all these strivings if not earthly profit, volatile fame, fleeting and impermanent desire, or the unsuitable and fickle favor of popular whims, which are more uncertain and more fleeting than any wind? Through so many and such rigorous convolutions they aspire to their goal. When they reach it, they will then rest. Meanwhile, according to Aristotelian teaching, they do not take time so that they may someday have time; that is, they work so that they may rest, and they work intensely so that they may enjoy a little rest; no truly, so they may have no rest at all; even more truly, so that they may work even more. So they are greatly deceived and, as it is said, they wander from the right way. Their leader deceives them, whether he is a philosopher or some advisor, and each person is deceived by his own hope and opinion that have become ingrained in himself. Certainly when one has labored greatly for a long time, whether he arrives at his destination or not, his labor only increases, and his worries double. The joy of success for which one has hoped usually leads to an accumulation of worries no less than does the pain of failure. So we should say more properly that they do not take time now, and therefore they will never have any time at all.

How much better and more secure the advice I bring to you; nay, certainly not I, but the prophet of God; no, rather God Himself. For He speaks in this way: "Take time and know that I am God."[9] Who is so rebellious to a human command or so unbelieving that he does not both tremble to hear the voice of God and submissively receive the lesson of Him Who declares "I am God"? Take time, for this is the advice, or more truly the lesson, which is imposed upon us. Take time, I say. This is the command of Him Whom it is not right to resist, Whom no one can flee or avoid, unless in fleeing a peaceful God he may encounter an angry God. Take time now so that you may take time forever; rest for the present so that you may rest for eternity, a hope which another psalm offers to us: "Sleep in peace to this end, and rest."[10] For what else is "Take time and know"? "Take time": this means there is rest in the present; "know" means there will be eternal repose. Take time on earth, and you will know in heaven. Even on earth the eye is able to know, insofar as it is pure and cleansed, but still carnal. This is an amazing thing, absolutely unique, and much more beneficial than other human affairs.

Among other people labor creates more labor; among you, however, rest creates rest. No such valuable reward has ever been purchased for such a low price. Prepare your minds. Give your right hands in pledge. With all zeal beware not to miss such a fortunate opportunity. Do you seek peace for your soul? Nothing is demanded of you except that you find repose in your spirit. Rest will give you rest, a goal which untiring and resolute minds ought to have worked toward through their whole lives. No labor would have appeared heavy if it had resulted in something so enjoyable as rest.

Now you are in no way ordered to do anything except to do no work and to learn to rest now so that you may rest forever, nor if you love that rest in the hereafter, must you scorn rest on earth, which in and of itself is sweet and leads to a level, straight, safe, and delightful path toward the most blessed repose that awaits.

Take time, my brothers. The lesson is short and not difficult. You are not commanded to fight, to sail, to plow, to be ambitious, to accumulate gold, fame, vain knowledge, all instruments of desire. They are useless, harmful, lethal. They are costly. They are sought with labor. Once attained, they do not satisfy us. When lost, they torture us. Having to be guarded, they worry us. In their midst we are never at peace: everywhere there is fear, everywhere there is labor.

There is one very safe, very useful, very easy lesson: you should take time. "Take time," he says; the fact that he has added "know" can be considered not so much another lesson as the reward of the first lesson. All in all, who is so frail that he is not able to excel in this task: to rest? Certainly if any of those things which mortals pursue were commanded, each man would be able to claim as excuses for himself the weakness of his body or mind, employment, impediments, inexperience, or ignorance. Now what excuse on earth has been left since nothing is commanded except this one thing: Take time?

Is there perhaps someone who could not accomplish either of these commands? Indeed, if the words of Horace are commonly enough known: "Nothing is a challenge for mortals."[11] Nevertheless, many matters are not only difficult or challenging, but impossible and completely beyond human capacity.

Who is not able to take time? This fellow fears the seas, that one avoids anxiety, another fears swords and dust, still another flees study or labor, but who, I ask you, fears rest except the man who hates himself? So take time, for by taking time you will certainly rest, and by resting you will know, and by knowing you will rejoice, and indeed, "by rejoicing about the truth,"[12] you will be happy. There is no happiness more certain than that, none more sublime. Even those men, to whom true rest, perfect vision, and the real cause of each are unknown, affirm that by resting, the soul does indeed become wise, a capacity which resides especially in being able to observe.

Alas for wretched and blind mortals! There is the sort of man who both loves work and fears and hates rest. We have read about that old man who was not forced to keep working. He ought to have been fatigued by his long life and ought to have needed rest. Considering the man's age, the emperor ordered him to retire, forbade him to work, cut him off from public business, and prohibited him from the senate house, the source of his toils. But that old man, who should have been grateful, was hurt, complained, and wept for himself for a long time, as if he were dead, until the man who had ordered him to rest restored the stupid old fellow to his labors and his cares. Clearly we, who have read of this one man, have seen how many old men act as he did: neither reason nor extreme old age ever diverted them from the complexities of affairs and from laborious business unless it was against their will, but even then they blamed the injustice of this greatest benefit of nature!

Then what St. Augustine says in his book *Of True Religion* is certainly true: "The friends of this world so fear to be separated from its embrace that nothing for them is more laborious than not to work."[13] So whoever is such a person, let him go from here and let him run along after his pleasures, expecting to find there enough of what he seeks, and let him hear this saying for himself: "He will labor forever and he will not die."[14] That is, he will not even rest from his labors in death, which is the one end of all visible labors, but he will live forever, not so that he may live, but rather that he may work. For thus says a certain interpreter of that text: "Those without piety might wish to die, but they cannot; therefore, they live so that they may die, for just as the life of the saints is eternal, so also is the death of the impious." These are in fact the words of Augustine. Thus by necessity every person who is greedy for work will labor for eternity, and although he may die in body, yet he will live in spirit, a thing which not even philosophers of the Gentiles deny. They are certainly ignorant of the fact, however, that he will come back to life in his body for punishment. Whole and fresh, the very same person, not someone else, he will still live for this very purpose of being tortured without end and of working for eternity, with his wish fulfilled and no reason to complain. It shall be said to him: Why are you sad, "why do you gnash your teeth,"[15] or why do you weep? You have found what you were seeking. You have acquired what you wanted. You were afraid to take time and to rest. Now work! You have no need here ever to seek labor or fear rest. Just go on, run everywhere, file lawsuits, argue, struggle, shout, fight, work in all ways. Nobody dissuades you; nobody prohibits you. You have those as your companions who are delighted by such things and who once offered you the opportunity to be delighted by them too.

What do you think? These people will not allow you to rest, even if you wanted to. As that same Augustine says in the same book, but in another place: "Wretched are those for whom the familiar loses value and who rejoice in novelties: they learn things more readily than they know them, although knowledge is the result of learning. Wretched too are those who despise liberty of action: they fight more readily than they win, although victory is the result of fighting."[16] I pass over in silence those things which follow, for I recall that I have written them in that book which I have recently published, *The Life of Solitude,* which is closely related to this book both in material and in style. The former precedes the latter in time and the order of considerations, but all our points aim at one conclusion, that it is the badge of mortal madness which rejoices more in work than in the enjoyment of work.

Otherwise, pressing on to reveal what lies between the erroneous and perverse intentions of these men and the holy and sober intentions of the just, not much later Augustine says: "Therefore those [of the latter group] who desire these very results are first of all free of curiosity. Knowing that certain knowledge is within, they profit from it as much as they can in this life. Then, putting aside obstinacy, they obtain liberty of action, knowing that the better and easier victory is not to resist the wrath of anyone, and they hold to this opinion as much as they can in this life."[17] Then a bit later he says: "After this life, however, our understanding will be perfected because now we know only in part, but when that which is perfect comes, it will not be just in part, but all peace and all health will be with us. Neither need nor fatigue will affect the body because when the resurrection of the flesh shall take place, the corruptible body will be clothed in incorruptibility in its due time and order. No wonder then that these men love peace when in action and seek health alone in their body, for that which they love more in this life will be perfected in them after this life."[18]

Because you have subjected your flesh to the spirit as much as is possible for mankind, you can garner the utmost hope from these words of Augustine, who twists the continual attack of his pen against those carnal men whom I had begun to discuss: "Some people, therefore, make

such poor use of this great gift of the mind that they are more attracted to
those things outside the mind which ought to have invited them to see
and love the intelligibles.[19] Those people will be thrown into the farthest
shadows of hell, and those who now delight in struggles will be deprived
of peace and entangled in the greatest difficulties. The beginning of the
greatest difficulty is war and contention, and this, I think, is signified by
the fact that their hands and feet are bound, that is, all ease of functioning is taken away."[20] Not content with these words, purposefully pro-
longing that conversation which he had begun, he says "For there are
many people who love all these incitements to vice at the same time and
whose joy it is to see spectacles, eat, drink, satisfy the flesh, sleep, and
embrace in their own thoughts nothing other than the fantasies which
arise from such a life. From their fallacious belief or impiety they form
rules which deceive them and to which they cling, even if they should try
to abstain from the attractions of the flesh, because they do not make
good use of the talent entrusted to them, that is, the mental acuity with
which those who are called learned, urbane, or witty all seem to excel,
but their mental acuity is tied in a handkerchief or hidden in the earth,
that is, wrapped up and overwhelmed by voluptuous and superfluous
matters or by earthly desires.

"Therefore their hands and feet will be bound, and they will be cast
into the farthest shadows. In that place there will be wailing and gnash-
ing of teeth, not because they have loved these things — for who loves
them? — but because those things which they have loved were the causes
of those torments and by necessity led their lovers to such torments.
Indeed, those who prefer to journey rather than to return home ought to
be sent to distant places because their flesh and spirit are always moving,
never coming back."[21]

Having borrowed these words from Augustine selectively, I omit
many things lest the greater part of the work which I have undertaken should not be my own, although words which have been sought
with long zeal and great cost of time should not seem someone else's.
These worthwhile and splendid sayings should not belong to individuals, but (as it pleases Seneca) they should be "public expressions."[22]
I have, of course, included more willingly and abundantly those words
which appeared to pertain to the matter so that I might show that
those men who labored very eagerly and more than necessary in this
life will also labor forever in that life which awaits. They will live for

this purpose, as I was saying, that there may be no hope of ending labor with death. I would also show that either the joy or the punishment of those things which delight each man while he is alive is reserved for him after his death.

This is true not only for Christians, for whom it is written in the book of Wisdom, "that they may know that in whatever way any man sins, in that way he shall also be punished,"[23] but the Gentile poets as well, since the most outstanding of them hid on remote footpaths in the underworld the souls of lovers whose "cares do not relinquish their hold in death itself."[24] The same poet, assigning the souls of warriors to their own places when he made them exercise their limbs and wrestle on a grassy plot, concluded: "Their spears stand fixed in the ground, and everywhere horses graze loose through the plain. Whatever pleasure the living had in chariots and in weapons, whatever concern for grazing sleek horses, the same follows them when they have been buried in the earth."[25] Although the writer may have arbitrarily invented these words, yet so great a man as he would not have imagined such things unless it was a common opinion. According to the variety of desires manifested in this life, he imagined that different conditions of souls remained after death, but this condition would be especially similar to that which each man enjoyed while alive. This is an opinion which you will see confirmed by Augustine, albeit with other words such as are fitting for a pious and holy man, when he asserts without hesitation that those men who delight in strife are to be kept away from peace and are to be involved in the greatest hardships. If I consider this, what more need I say, brothers, except that which has often been stated and must be repeated more often: "Take time."

❧   ❧   ❧

NOTES

1. Suetonius, *Lives of the Caesars,* Julius 37. Citations follow standard English editions, when available. Cf. Petrarch, *On Famous Men* 2.568.

2. Jer. 1:5, Petrarch's references are to the Vulgate version of the Bible. For the Psalms he relies on the Septuagint version of the Vulgate.

3. Ps. 45:11.

4. Gen. 29:20.

5. Jacob served Laban for fourteen years in order to marry his beloved Rachel.

6. Ps. 22:1-2, 36:5, 39:18, 54:23.

7. Aristotle, *Nichomachean Ethics* 1177b.

8. Vergil, *Aeneid* 1.91.

9. Ps. 45:11.

10. Ps. 4:9.

11. Horace, *Odes* 1.3.37.

12. 1 Cor. 13:6.

13. Augustine, *Of True Religion* 35.65. This early work by Augustine (354–430), the greatest of the Latin Church Fathers, was one of Petrarch's favorite books and a key text for understanding Petrarch's *Secret.*

14. Ps. 48:9-10.

15. Ps. 111:10.

16. Augustine, *Of True Religion* 53-54.

17. Ibid.

18. Ibid.

19. The intelligibles are the forms or essences of created beings as found in the mind of God.

20. Augustine, *Of True Religion* 53-54.

21. Ibid.

22. Seneca, Letter to Lucan, *Epistles* 3 and 59.

23. Wisd. 11:17.

24. Vergil, *Aeneid* 6.444.

25. Ibid. 652-55.

2

Now by chance someone among us, a man of good will, but not as well educated as the rest, may ask: "From which of our concerns, my friend, shall we take our rest?" It is surely not right for those who profess to fight for Christ to rest from all that has to be done. I am not encouraging you to inactivity, but rather just to be at leisure, and that for religious purposes.

Enjoy leisure from those superfluous tasks which wear out our body and spirit, from the carnal desires which defile and weaken our whole person, from the visual lusts which deflect us from the acquisition of knowledge, from the ambitions of this age which ensnare us with their claws and shackles, from useless concerns which inflame our heart with unseen torches, and finally from all sins which torture, oppress, and destroy our unhappy soul.

In the midst of all of this, take time. Relinquish not only the harmful memory of time past, which keeps drawing us back even when we are no longer there and arouses long-dormant longings in us, but also all memory of previous good deeds, for lethargy mixed with confidence corrupts minds which are conscious of having done well. Think rather with the Apostle Paul, "forgetting those things which are in the past, but straining forward to that which is ahead, pursue them to the goal, to the reward of the heavenly summons of God in Jesus Christ."[1] Fulfill in yourselves what you praise in St. Anthony, about whom it is written that "he did not set a value on the merits of his own labors by the length of time spent, but on love and spontaneous service. Just as if he were always standing in the presence of God, the fear of God incited him to progress because he desired to supplement his former merits with new ones."[2] He always kept before his eyes both that saying of the Apostle cited above and that prophecy of Elijah: "The Lord Whom I serve today is alive,"[3] where "'today' would be an appropriate word because Elijah was not calculating past time, but if he were assigned a post of battle everyday, he wanted to present himself as the sort of person who he knew was worthy of the sight of God."[4]

Show yourselves, therefore, to be this sort of man in the eyes of Him Who watches you, as men who foresee future danger, who forget the past and its burdens, and who are unconcerned with rewards. If there is any worldly care enticing you even now from the rear, if there is any gently whispering hint of this alluring world following you, clothe yourselves in the remedies of the Scriptures. I have no need to collect these since Augustine has already completed the labor of collecting them for us.

He says, "This is said to those who are greedy: Do not bury treasures for yourselves, where moth and rust destroy and where thieves dig up and steal, but lay away treasures for yourselves in heaven where neither moth nor rust destroy and where thieves do not dig, for where your treasure is, there also is your heart."[5]

This is written for those who love luxury: "He who plants in the flesh shall reap corruption from the flesh; he who plants in the spirit will reap eternal life from the spirit."

And to the proud: "He who raises himself up shall be humbled."

This is spoken to those who are easily angered: "Have you received a slap on the face? Offer the other cheek."

For those who cause trouble: "Love your enemies."

This is said to those who are superstitious: "The kingdom of God is within you."

And to those who quest: "Do not seek those things which are visible, but those which are not seen, for those things which are seen are temporal, but what are not seen are eternal."

Finally this is said to all people: "Love neither this world nor those things which are in this world, because every worldly thing involves the desire of the flesh and the desire of the eyes and the striving of this world."[6]

So Augustine has expounded upon these things and has warned us, but infinite other words of this sort have been spoken for the consolation and guidance of our souls. Indeed, this is written to those who are worried: "Have no care for tomorrow; have no care for your life, for what you should eat, nor what you should wear on your body: your Father knows that you need these things."[7] Rather "seek the kingdom of God, and all these things will be given to you."[8]

For those who are unstable and without direction: "Take my yoke upon you."[9]

To those who lack pity he says, "Learn from me that I am gentle and humble in heart."[10]

This is said to those who hope for long life: "Fool, this very night they come to get your soul from you. All those things, however, which you have prepared, whose will they be?"[11]

This is said to those who desire power and greatness: "What benefit is it for a man if he should gain the whole world, but suffer the loss of his soul?"[12]

There are words for those who are exalted, rapacious, and inordinately rich: "Do not hope in wickedness and do not lust for plunder. If your riches increase, do not set your heart on them"[13]; and "Teach the rich of this age: do not be proud and place no hope in the uncertainty of riches, but in the living God, Who places before us in abundance all things to be enjoyed. Teach them to live well, to become rich in good deeds, to be generous, to share, to store up a treasure for themselves as a good foundation for the future so that they may acquire true life."[14]

We hear these words spoken to those who love their wealth too much, hoping in it and not putting "God their helper"[15] in His proper place: "All men of wealth have finished their sleep and have found nothing in their hands."[16]

To those who are swollen with temporal self-importance and forgetful of the human condition: "O God of Jacob, those who rode horses have fallen asleep at Your rebuke. You are terrifying, and who will stand against You?"[17] Do not forget that equally terrifying line of the other prophet: "If you are exalted like an eagle, and if you put your nest among the stars, I shall pull you down from there, says the Lord."[18]

This is written to those who are not content with moderation: "Give me neither poverty nor wealth; give only that which is necessary for my nourishment lest by chance I become satiated and led to deny You and ask 'Who is God?,' lest driven by need, I rage and perjure the name of my God."[19] And "Piety together with contentment is a great advantage, for we have brought nothing into this world, nor without doubt are we able to take anything with us; having food and covering, we are content with these things. Those who want to become rich fall into temptation, into the noose of the devil, and into many useless and harmful desires which thrust mankind into destruction and ruin. For love of money is the root of all evils, and those who seek money have indeed strayed from their faith and have involved themselves in many sorrows."[20]

On the other hand, however, the poor hear this: "Blessed are the poor in spirit, for theirs is the kingdom of heaven."[21]

The rich, however, read: "Woe to you who are rich, for you will be hungry."[22]

Conversely, however, we read this to those who hunger and thirst: "Blessed are those who hunger and thirst for justice, for they themselves will be satisfied."[23] And again: "If anyone thirsts, let him come to me and let him drink."[24]

For those who tastelessly ridicule others: "Woe to you who laugh now, for you will mourn and weep."[25]

On the other hand, this is said to those who mourn: "Blessed are those who mourn, for they themselves will be consoled."[26]

Lest they suffer doubt, this is spoken to those who endure persecution: "All those who wish to live dutifully in Christ Jesus will endure persecution,"[27] and again, lest they be disheartened: "Blessed are those who endure persecution in the name of justice, for theirs is the kingdom of heaven."[28]

To the weary and oppressed one may read: "Come to me, you who labor and have been burdened, and I will restore you."[29]

To young men filled with lust: "Youth and lust are meaningless."[30]

Those who rejoice and think that this is the only life will hear it said: "Light is sweet: it is delightful to see the sun with your eyes. If a person has lived many years and has been happy in all of them, he ought to remember the shadowy time and the many days ahead which, when they arrive, will expose his past of vanity. So be happy, young man, in your youth, let your heart be happy in the days of your youth, walk in the ways of your heart and whatever your eyes see, and know that in return for all these things God will lead you to judgment."[31]

This is said to those without motivation for good works: "Go to the ant, O lazy one, consider its ways, and learn wisdom: although the ant has neither a guide nor a teacher nor a chief, he prepares food for himself during the summer and accumulates in the harvest that which he will eat. How long will you sleep and be lazy? When will you rise from your sleep? You will sleep a little while, you will slumber for a little while, you will fold your hands a little so that you may sleep. Need will come to you like a visitor, and poverty will come like an armed man, but if you have been energetic, your harvest will come like a fountain, and need will flee far from you."[32]

Those who are depressed and sad as well hear these words: "You should not give grief to your soul nor afflict yourself in your thoughts. The pleasure of the heart is human life and the treasure in which sanctity resides. Human happiness celebrates in longevity. Take pity on your soul as you continue to please God, and restrain yourself; place your heart in His sanctity and drive grief far from you, for grief kills many people and is of no use. Jealousy and wrath will lessen your days, and worry will bring old age before its time."[33]

This is for drunkards and gluttons: "How sufficient is a little wine to a learned man: while you sleep, you will not suffer from it, nor will you feel pain. The immoderate man will suffer wakefulness, stomach disorders, and torment. The sober man will enjoy a healthy sleep: he will sleep until morning, and his soul will be delighted in him."[34] "What is life when it is lessened by wine? From the beginning wine has been created for pleasure, not for drunkenness. Wine drunk moderately is the joy of the soul and the heart; it is the health of the soul and the sober drink of the body. Wine drunk in excess causes irritation, anger, and widespread destruction."[35] Paul said, "Do not get drunk on an excess of wine."[36] Consider this from the prophet Joel: "Wake up, drunkards, and weep. All you who drink wine, wail in its sweetness because it has been withheld from your mouth."[37]

This is said to those who have forgotten the justice of God: "Understand, all you who forget God, lest He take you away some day and there be nobody who can take you back."[38]

This is written to those who make excuses for their faults and deflect them onto God: "Let not your heart indulge in malicious words to justify your excuses for sinning."[39] And "I have now discovered this one thing, that God has made humanity upright, and he has enveloped himself in infinite schemes."[40]

It is said to those presuming they are just and innocent: "There is not a just man on earth who does good and does not sin."[41] And "If we have said that we have no fault, we are fooling ourselves, and there is no truth in us."[42]

It is said to those who despair of their sin: "If we should confess our sins, He is faithful and just, so He will forgive us."[43] And this as well: "Not in accordance with our sins has He acted toward us, nor in accordance with our injustices will He repay us, for He has strengthened his mercy for those who fear Him according to the height of heaven from earth. He has removed our sins from us as far as east stands from west."[44]

Indeed, we read this, spoken to a paralyzed man: "Lift up your cot and walk. Lo, you have been made whole; now do not sin any more lest something worse should happen to you."[45]

This He said to one who had a shriveled hand: "Stretch out your hand."[46]

This He said to a leper: "Be cleansed; it is my wish."[47] This is spoken to a blind man: "See again, your faith has saved you,"[48] and immediately the former was cleansed; the latter saw and "followed Him giving praise to God."[49]

This He said to a dead man: "Young man, I say to you, rise,"[50] and instantly he rose and spoke. Similarly, so neither sex would lose faith in the Resurrection, He spoke in a similar fashion to a dead girl: "Girl, rise,"[51] and straightway her spirit returned and she rose up. Finally He said to the man already stinking from four days in the tomb: "Lazarus, come forth,"[52] and more quickly than that command, he came forth from his tomb, bound head, foot, and hand, just as he was.

These words are spoken generally to those who are in utter need of everything: "Ask and it will be given to you, seek and you will find, knock and it will be opened to you, for every person who asks receives, every person who seeks finds, and the door is opened to one who knocks."[53]

One who has lost faith hears this: "O man of little faith, why have you doubted?"[54] To the person who feels regret He says: "Thus there will be greater joy in heaven when a single sinner repents than for ninety-nine just men who do not need repentance."[55] And again: "We had to feast and rejoice because your brother had died and has come back to life; he was lost and has been found."[56]

To those who restrain their passions He said: "There are eunuchs who have castrated themselves for the kingdom of heaven: let him accept this who can."[57]

This is said expressly to you who have left the world behind: "Everyone who has left his home or brothers or sisters or father or mother or sons or fields for My name's sake will be paid a hundred times over and will possess eternal life."[58] And again: "Fear not, tiny flock, because it has pleased your Father to give a kingdom to you."[59]

This is spoken to those who haughtily spout philosophy and rant against those ideas expressed above: "Do not raise your horn up high; do not speak iniquity against God."[60] The insolence of philosophers is repressed by the words of one who is not only a prophet, but a woman: "Do not brag in order to inflate your speech with lofty accomplishments; let your old words depart from your mouth, for God is the master of knowledge, and thoughts are prepared through Him."[61]

What am I doing? Is there any corner of the Scriptures anywhere which is not full of useful threats and admonitions, which is not full of consolations and cures for the soul? Therefore take time, my brothers, from these unseen plagues about which I have warned you above and am about to speak further, and so that I may settle the matter once and for all, abstain from all matters in which the peril of your soul lies.

NOTES

1. Phil. 3:13-14.

2. Athanasius, *Life of St. Anthony* 6. St. Anthony was born at Komo on the Nile about 250 and died in 356. He is regarded as the founder of the anchoritic life. Athanasius, bishop of Alexandria (295–373), was a staunch opponent of Arius. See also *Patrologia Latina* (PL) 73.131.

3. 3 Kings (1 Reg.) 18:15.

4. Athanasius, *Life of St. Anthony* 6.

5. Augustine, *Of True Religion* 3.4; paraphrasing Matt. 6:19-21.

6. Augustine, *Of True Religion* 3.4.

7. Matt. 6:34, 25.

8. Matt. 6:32-33.

9. Matt. 11:29.

10. Ibid.

11. Luke 12:20.

12. Matt. 16:26.

13. Ps. 61:11.

14. 1 Tim. 6:17-19.

15. Ps. 51:9.

16. Ps. 75:6.

17. Ps. 75:7-8.

18. Obad. 4.

19. Prov. 30:8-9.

20. 1 Tim. 6:6-10.

21. Matt. 5:3.

22. Luke 6:25.

23. Matt. 5:6.

24. John 7:37.

25. Luke 6:25.

26. Matt. 5:5.

27. 2 Tim. 3:12.

28. Matt. 5:10.

29. Matt. 11:28.

30. Eccles. 11:10.

31. Eccles. 11:7-9.
32. Prov. 6:6-11.
33. Ecclus. 30:22-26.
34. Ecclus. 31:22-24.
35. Ecclus. 31:33-38.
36. Eph. 5:18.
37. Joel 1:5.
38. Ps. 49:22.
39. Ps. 140:4.
40. Eccles. 7:30.
41. Eccles. 7:21.
42. 1 John 1:8.
43. 1 John 1:9.
44. Ps. 102:10-12.
45. John 5:8, 11, 14.
46. Luke 6:10.
47. Luke 5:13 and Matt. 8:3.
48. Luke 18:42.
49. Luke 18:43.
50. Luke 7:14.
51. Mark 5:41.
52. John 11:43.
53. Matt. 7:7-8.
54. Matt. 14:31.
55. Luke 15.7.
56. Luke 15:32.
57. Matt. 19:12.
58. Matt. 19:29.
59. Luke 12:32.
60. Ps. 74:6.
61. 1 Kings 2:3.

3

Do not love danger. It is written: "Whoever loves danger will perish in it."[1] Do not "seek" some frequently dubious "proof"[2] of your-selves. These are the skills of our adversary. Do not let him drag you to some perilously steep place because of the hope you put in your own strengths. A man is usually said to have too much self-confidence and to lift his over-confident soul too high above him with the result that he may be ashamed when he has realized that he has been deluded and has fallen shy of his undertaking, even to the extent of abandoning easy tasks. This failure is fol-lowed by a reluctance to act boldly, a certain sluggishness, and (worst of all) a hatred of life and a sense of desperation for one's life. Avoid this pitfall and these deceptions; give your souls to Christ and bear his yoke with faithful necks: nothing is sweeter. To Him "give service in fear and exult in Him with trembling."[3] If this lesson was directed to kings and to the proud rulers of the earth, how much more is such instruction understood by the humble ser-vants of Christ! Remember His commandments and the pact made with Him on that day when you deserted the secular world and fled to His reign. Make sure you keep your commitment before your eyes, guard your vow, and fulfill your holy orders; if you do this joyfully, it is enough.

As for everything else, a dangerous temptation has often been linked to virtue. A man who does what he must at the extreme limit of his power in any matter concerning his body or his soul will quickly cease his efforts. We know that unusual effort can never be but a step away from exhaustion. With all your watchfulness protect your heart, and with constant determination beware those things which you recognize as ruinous. This will be easy for those who have experienced in the world what has been treacherous, violent, and especially threatening to your way of life. Cautiously avoid those things which you have understood to be more harmful: anger tortured one man, lust another; pride exalted one man, melancholy depressed another; greed, gluttony, and grievous jealousy aroused one man to a frenzy. Each man should recognize his own particular enemy in the battle, and then he should be especially aware of where the greater danger lies.

You should not think yourselves safe because you live in the camp of Christ, for although you may fight under the best leader and your camp may be very well fortified and very strong, nevertheless no place must be considered completely safe, for sleepless wild enemies make noise on all sides. No place is safe unless in front of the battlements there are armed watchmen, alert in mind and body, who keep watch against the attacks and treacheries of the enemy. Where should I search for such guards if I shall not have found them among you? Or about whom (if not about you) did Isaiah say: "Over your walls, Jerusalem, I have put guards. All day and all night they will never be silent in praising the name of the Lord."[4] I know your watches and your sentinels, which have brought me to tears, especially when I, such a great sinner both recently and earlier, am mindful that you were not at all in the number of those men about whom it has been said: "These people honor me with their lips, but their heart is far from me."[5] You, however, love much more with your heart than with your lips.

True virtue has this capacity: it arouses minds; it stimulates feelings; and just as distinguished virtue of mind makes even the tongue of a stutterer agreeable, so if the reputation of virtue is lacking, even Demosthenes speaking about virtue will not be pleasing. Your heavenly praises, however, soothe me, I confess, no less than if some sinner with great skill or if Aristoxenus[6] himself were to resound in my ear. Certainly the devotion of your mind is equivalent to the sweetness of music; I seem to have spoken well because your devotion exceeds my capacity to capture it. Returning frequently to this thought, I sometimes fear that my words, such as they are, have less authority and credibility, that the author's fickleness diminishes the importance of the matter, that I deserve to hear what the man born blind heard when given sight by God: "You have been born completely in sin, and you want to teach us?"[7] Like him I too will be cast forth. Your love, however, lessens this worry of mine, as does your simplicity in Christ, which judges no one and is prepared to hear what I say rather than to consider how I live.

I return to my point about you: even if your seclusion, vigil, and wakefulness should seem to keep you safe from all danger, you still have to be very watchful and prepared for everything. You may hope to have complete security and guaranteed peace when, having courageously and successfully completed your military life, you will be taken from this exile into your homeland, from military camps into the kingdom and into the palace of the true King. At that time you will be transformed from diligent soldiers into veterans who have served with distinction and have been rewarded for their past service.

Meanwhile, do not be too confident. There will be no end of dangers until the end of life. Always look around and stand like helmeted and armored soldiers with swords drawn in a battle line, and do not let this assignment tax such outstanding warriors. However great this labor may be, it will not be as great as its reward. You will not fight for more than — I shall not say not longer than one Olympiad[8] compared to a thousand years — but not more than one day, a brief one at that, compared to eternity. So act for the King of heaven and for your own salvation. Do that which most mortals have done for their earthly masters and for a small amount of money; you know your enemy very well, a fact which has been the cause of victory for many people. Indeed, in every war it is best to know what the enemy are doing and what they can do, for sudden actions terrify us, and unforeseen occurrences disturb us. Caution is easier against anticipated assaults, and whatever you have foreseen from afar approaches with less threat.

Therefore, know your enemies, what they are plotting, and what they think. Oppose their wicked devices, especially three kinds of weapons of the enemy: the traps of this world, the enticements of the flesh, and the guiles of demons. The first promises things which are insubstantial; the next lures one as an old friend, but the last whisper their worst counsels to mortals. It all depends on one thing, that you take time, concentrating on this one idea: to remove your mind from all fellowship with such enemies, lest unforeseen they fall upon you when you happen to be involved in something else. The world fools you, the flesh allures you, demons drive you on. From the first you have no hope, from the second no pleasure, from the last no counsel. They are all conspiring equally for your ruin and death.

I begin with the last although I may trust that there is not one of these invisible enemies who does not shudder at your life, your habit, and your dwelling. Nevertheless, why should I think there is nothing to be feared? The devil has not feared the threshold of paradise, but having entered and guilefully attacked man, who was made in the image of God and by His own hand, he conquered him, laid him low, drove him out, and thrust him into exile and death. What am I saying? Indeed, how little effort was it for him, who has tempted Christ our Lord, to deceive Adam? Surely there is nothing he does not dare to do. Pride and jealousy spur him on, but he plots against no one more than against the servants of Christ, for who has greater happiness, and of what place can he be more envious? So take time and stay away from all the advice of demons and their leader, for "he is a liar and the father of falsehood."9 That is what the Living Truth calls him, and whoever will admit him into his company will find him to be just that. He daily proposes many things to the ear of the heart. Close that ear, turn away, and cut off his impure and seductive tongue. Do not tremble. Christ brings help to His own soldiers who struggle on the battle line; otherwise, beyond all doubt, they would fail from the exhaustion of fighting so many wars. The Psalmist says, "I always had the Lord in my sight because He is on my right hand so that I may not lose courage."10 See Him before you. He is always at your right hand, He is nearby for you, just as He is for all who call upon Him: not to all who say "Lord, Lord," but to all who call upon Him in truth.

The unlucky man who has driven Him away is deservedly going to suffer what another psalm says, that is, "let the devil stand at his right hand."11 Flee this destructive exchange. You have clothed yourselves in our Lord Jesus Christ and His armor.12 You have affixed the banner of His cross to your foreheads. You have sworn in the name of Christ. You have declared on Satan a war which long ago from the beginning of the human race that fiend had already declared on you. You have a Leader, the sight of Whose sign alone, the sound of Whose sacred name, His enemies are not strong enough to endure. It is impossible for you to be conquered in this battle unless you agree to it. Let no one agree, let no one flee from the victor to the vanquished, from a powerful leader to a weak one, from the best to the worst.

In secular histories we read that Labienus was scorned because he had gone over to Pompey's side, leaving victorious Caesar behind.13 Although the decision of fortune between those factions is obvious enough, an understanding of the reasons for Caesar's victory are still difficult to establish. How much more justly must a man be scorned who has deserted our most victorious king Christ and has fled to that foe whose custom is to tempt. Why should someone who resists him and bears his first attack suffer defeat and flee? Thus it has been written: "Resist the devil, and he will flee from you."14 A memorable piece of advice, my brothers, nor is that advice any less memorable which is written in the same passage: "Approach God and He will approach you."15 We ought to embrace both counsels with our whole soul and bind them to us so that we may drive off the perfidious foe by resisting him and hold on to our devoted Lord by approaching Him. We must pursue and acknowledge His grace, not with our feet, but with our heart, just as the martyr Grisantus is said to have responded to the tribune Claudius, who was at that time the administrator of imperial cruelty and who would soon undergo martyrdom for the name of Christ: "For God is only present to each person to the extent that he has sought Him with the faith of his mind and the integrity of his heart."[16]

Obviously this is an obligation, not only for all humanity, but also especially for you. Although all other people who rejoice in the name of Christ have undergone the rebirth of holy baptism only once, you have renounced your adversary both at that time and again in your vow of holy religion. Persevere faithfully now, you have left his camp whose "reward is death"[17] and have happily converted to Christ's victorious standards.

Nothing more troublesome can happen to the enemy. The devil certainly grieves, rages, and is angered, but what is he to do? He can do nothing more than that which the opposing Leader allows him to do. Therefore, keep up your hopes and by all means be calm. Certainly Christ has permitted nothing at any time against His followers, in whose battle line you march, nor will He permit anything unless it is for their well-being and salvation.

That person is exceptionally weak who can do nothing except what his enemy wants: indeed Satan constantly and repeatedly makes many attempts, and he struggles in vain and rages uselessly, and in the midst of his effort he reins in his treachery. Of course, he tries whatever he is allowed so that we may not relax in tranquil peace, but be alert and recognize the source of fearful treacheries against which we must be on guard, as well as the source from which we are to seek and hope for help. We learn, consequently, not to rely on ourselves in anything, but to lift up "our eyes unto the mountains from which help shall come to us."[18] Our help, however, will come not from the mountains, but from the Lord "Who made heaven and earth."[19]

Military leaders are accustomed to send their soldiers into danger so that they can know their soldiers' courage and spirit, but our Leader is not like that. Indeed, He is One Who has known us before the beginning of time, but that is why He trains us to know ourselves and not to attribute blindly and ungratefully to ourselves the things which are His.

Marcus Tullius Cicero said it very well in this passage: "O immortal gods," he said, "I shall attribute to you the things which are yours."[20] What could be more religious or more pleasing? In general, what could be more modest? Had he only confessed that one "God," not "the gods," was the source of his thoughts and all the things which he did. Perhaps he might have done this if he had remembered that he himself had written that it was not fitting for a philosopher to speak of gods. It is my hope for Cicero's genius, however, that his mind remained on a solid foundation even if, because of some fear or habit of his mind, his tongue or his pen was forcefully overcome by a flood of popular misconceptions. I am convinced that this is true because, besides his natural mental acuity and inborn reason, by which "the invisible works of God are seen and understood through those things which have been made,"[21] as well as God's eternal power and divinity, he had learned from Plato that God was master of the world and from Plato's student Aristotle that God was the first principle of all things.

If, however, Cicero, a man of divine gifts, acknowledges and announces that the discovery, punishment, and repression of Catiline's conspiracy[22] was the work of "god" (a conspiracy, I confess, which was serious, deadly, and incited by a domestic enemy who was mortal and visible, to be sure), what will a Christian man say when on one side a familiar, mortal, and visible enemy readies himself to kill him, and on the other side an invisible and immortal enemy does the same? Ambrose says that an unseen infestation of demons or a multitude of thieves besieges the path of our life. On all the roads unseen subverters of souls stretch snares which must be feared as causes for the deaths of countless people. The Apostle Paul says: "You are not contending against flesh and blood, but against princes and powers, against the rulers of the shadows of this world, against the spiritual forces of evil in the heavens."[23] Even Augustine says in that book which I often call to witness today (for when one speaks about religious leisure, what could provide more appropriate support than his book *Of True Religion*?): "All power of men over men," he says, "ends with the death either of the masters or of the subjects, but slavery under the arrogance of fallen angels is especially frightening in the time which follows death. Moreover, it is easy for anyone to understand because one has the right to have free thoughts under a human master, but fear of these other masters dominates our very minds."[24] It is our task, therefore, to ward off from our battlements those who are not masters, but the haughtiest tyrants who climb up even to the very citadel of our mind, to discover the plot of these fiends and of our flesh, a plot which is hidden under a cloud of passing pleasure. It is our task to avoid this plot and hold it in check.

Would it not be a magnificent gift of divine grace that the person, to whom this happened, might make that Ciceronian expression his own? "O immortal God, for to You shall I attribute those things which are Yours."[25] Let him also say what follows: "Nor truly can I give credit only to my own genius that I have on my own perceived so many great, different, and unexpected things in that very turbulent storm."[26] You, O God, certainly have set fire to my mind with the desire of saving my soul. You have brought me from all other thoughts to the one thought of salvation. Finally, in the midst of such great shadows of error and ignorance, You have illuminated my mind with a brilliant light. We ought to turn these words of Cicero to our own advantage, with very little alteration to suit the situation, so that with such an authority we may learn to recognize the salvation of our soul and the victory over an invisible enemy, both of which come from God.

In this opinion, in this hope, therefore, my brothers, persevere and let no man claim for himself that he has not sinned and that he has not found more than pardon for his sin. We have committed many sins for which we very obviously deserved death, had not divine grace come to our rescue. There is no sin which we could not commit if divine providence had not preserved us from such great evils. Never to have been sick and to have been cured of illness are both equally the gifts of God, just as never to have been miserable and to have earned mercy. We may wonder which is the greater gift. Indeed, the former seems to me to be the purer; the latter, however, more striking because of the very union of opposites and more pleasing because of the memory of danger.

Stand firm in this reverent and serious recognition of divine assistance; refer all your blessings back to that source from which all blessings come. I know for certain that those who are surrounded by such opinions can be invaded, but not overwhelmed, for if it would seem fitting to pious leisure never to be invaded, it is perhaps not completely beneficial for salvation. We must not hope for total security, for often that is the mother of apathy and thence of danger. In the long run, security is best when it is eternal, a condition which will not exist before one has reached the kingdom of God. Certainly, however, caution is the safe bet along this path which is so steep, so narrow, so covered with thorns, so slippery, blocked by so many obstacles, and besieged by so many petty robbers. Freedom from worry is suspect and may impede not only our spiritual, but also our worldly, journeys. I would like to know what sort of security it is which, while it appears to be more peaceful and more stable, can be interrupted by some sudden fear, an unforeseen disaster, or an unanticipated death.

That was known to the Apostle Paul: "The day of the Lord will come just like a thief in the night, for when people have said there is 'peace and security,' then a sudden destruction will come upon them."[27] You know the rest; and so that he may awaken your minds with this fear, he says, "So let us not sleep like the others do, but let us stay alert and be sober."[28] At any rate, he knew what sort of dangers freedom from concern brings with it. Who can count how many very powerful nations, not just individuals, such a lack of concern has destroyed?

I will be content with one single argument, and that same being well known. Allow me to recall for a moment examples from the pagan world. The Romans, who were surely the masters of all nations and the leaders without rival of this earthly state, were always glorious in their virtues and invigorated by constant use of arms out of fear of the Carthaginians and the frequency of their dangerous military encounters. Later, however, inactivity, born of security, covered those same Romans with the rust of vices. One man is said to have foreseen and predicted this: Scipio Nasica,[29] who at that time both was considered to be the best man in the state and was found to be wiser in this matter than Cato himself, who has a reputation for wisdom.[30] His opinions conform to the sayings of his other illustrious fellow-citizens too, Appius Claudius[31] and Quintus Metellus,[32] the former of whom said that "work is safer for the Roman people than leisure."[33] The latter dared to say in the senate after the defeat of Carthage that he did not know whether that victory was more useful or more disastrous for the Roman state if it diminished their military virtues to the degree that it added to their tranquility.[34]

Nor was any of them mistaken in as much as security, leisure, and rest overturned that warlike state's discipline and its glory, which fear and difficulty and hard work had kept vigorous. Not in jest the satirist poet wrote, "Now we suffer the evils of a long peace; luxury, which is more savage than weapons, has climbed into our beds and wreaks its vengeance on the conquered world."[35]

Perhaps it is not useful for you and your assembly to enjoy peace of all kinds, lest together with peace the companions of peace return: ill-conceived security, delicately soft feelings, and finally extravagance and vices. As long as this fragile warfare of life goes on, do not hope to be without an adversary, lest at the same time you lack both the challenge and the reward for your virtues. It was not without good reason that when St. Paul asked three times that the torment of his flesh should depart from him, meaning the fallen angel Satan who was assaulting him, he was told by that One Who alone knew what can set us free: "My grace is all you need," and "Virtue is perfected by infirmity."[36] Seek this grace and with the same Apostle find glory in your infirmity, which is the means for perfecting your virtue. Furthermore, so that the virtue of Christ may dwell in you, hope for war, certainly not for its own sake, but for the glory and eternal peace of Christ.

If that saying of Cicero is rightfully praised: "We must undertake wars with the result that we may live without injury in peace,"[37] and he is speaking about this life, which he elsewhere calls death, what should we think about the peace of that true and immortal life? Arm yourselves with the shield of long-suffering patience and of faith in this war which is certainly only temporary and just a preview of eternal peace; then nothing will have to be feared from your adversary. He will, however, never cease to wander about your sheep folds like a roaring lion and a famished wolf. He will inflict on you anxieties about your faith, and by them he may wound, delay, and impede your step as you hasten to your salvation.

※　※　※

NOTES

1. Ecclus. 3:27.
2. 2 Cor 13:3.
3. Ps. 2:11.
4. Isa. 62:6, 9.
5. Matt. 15:8.
6. Aristoxenus of Tarentum (fl. last quarter of the 4th century B.C.E.) was a disciple of Aristotle and specialized in music theory.
7. John 9:34.
8. The Greeks reckoned years as the first, second, third, or fourth year of a particular Olympiad, which was four years long. Thus what we call 776 B.C.E. was to them the first year of the first (recorded) Olympiad.
9. John 8:44. Cf. Dante, *Inferno* 23.144.
10. Ps. 15:8.
11. Ps. 108:6.
12. Cf. Eph. 6:11.
13. Labienus, initially a lieutenant of Julius Caesar during the Gallic wars, ultimately joined Pompey's faction in the civil war between Caesar and Pompey.
14. James 4:7.
15. James 4:8.
16. *Acts of the Saints,* Oct. 11.481.
17. Rom. 6:23.
18. Ps. 120:1.
19. Ps. 123:8.
20. Cicero, *On Behalf of Sulla* 40.
21. Rom. 1:20.
22. Cicero, *Against Catiline* 2.29, 3.22-23. Cicero, as consul of Rome in 63 B.C.E., foiled a plot led by Catiline to overthrow the Roman Republic.
23. Eph. 6:12.
24. Augustine, *Of True Religion* 55.111.
25. Cicero, *On Behalf of Sulla* 40.
26. Ibid.
27. 1 Thess. 5:2-3.
28. 1 Thess. 5:6.

29. Cf. Florus, 1.31.5., 2.15.

30. Marcus Porcius Cato ("the Elder"), who died 150 B.C.E., was famous for his strict morality.

31. Appius Claudius, consul of Rome in 397 and 396 B.C.E., urged the Senate not to make peace with Pyrrhus, the Epirote king who resisted Rome's advance into the Greek territory of Southern Italy.

32. Quintus Metellus led Roman armies against Hannibal in 207 and 206 B.C.E.

33. Valerius Maximus 7.2.1.

34. Valerius Maximus 7.2.3.

35. Juvenal, *Satires* 6.292-93.

36. 2 Cor. 12:9.

37. Cicero, *On Duties* 1.11.35.

4

Hear your King proclaiming: "If you do not believe in Me, believe in My accomplishments."[1] By all that is holy, if mortals have any faith, any hope of life, I approach these hardhearted people, who even now, cold in their belief, hesitate to accept a pledge of salvation, and mired in baseless superstition, are unable to spread the wings of faith by which the mind, wearied with corporeal mass, is lifted to heaven. I ask them whether they propose with adamantine harshness to believe in absolutely nothing or what they intend to believe.

If by chance someone may be so foolish to "say in his heart: 'There is no God,'"[2] I maintain that, although there may always have been a great and diverse difference of opinion because of the workings of the human mind, there was never a people so crude or inhuman that they did not believe in the existence of God. Even people who we have learned had no knowledge of the true God wanted to confirm this in their writings. Consequently, if one does not believe in Christ, in whom will he believe? in rocks? in ivory? in wood which is mute and lifeless, having a mouth but not speaking, having hands but not touching, having feet but not walking, having ears but not hearing, having nostrils but not smelling, having eyes but not seeing?[3] Isaiah says: "So in whose image have you made God, or what image will you put on Him? Will a smith forge some carved statue, or a goldsmith give it shape from gold and a silversmith from silver foil? Perhaps the skilled artisan has chosen incorruptible wood: he tries to determine how to make an idol stand upright and not be toppled over."[4] Even Horace once said sarcastically about this hardly incorruptible, but long disfigured and useless, wood: "A craftsman was unsure whether he should make a stool or a statue of Priapus. He preferred that it should be a god,"[5] more for frightening birds and thieves than for religion and the faithful, so that garden would have a protector rather than that the human mind have such a god.

Perhaps you wish to put your trust more securely instead in a more valuable metal, in silver and in gold, because "the graven images of nations are silver and gold, the works of human hands,"[6] by which "they may become similar to those who make them and all who trust in them."[7] Even in our own times we see many people, even Christians, believing in them. Shame and numbness seize the person who thinks about those gold and silver gods which ancient kings destroyed because they were instructed to do so by the words of holy priests out of reverence for Christ. To the detriment of Christ, however, they are now being eagerly rebuilt by our kings and priests.

We are lucky because they do not worship gold and silver as gods and, as that poet says in his biting style, "because money, cause of woe, does not yet live in heaven, nor have we erected altars of coins."[8] Nevertheless, they worship silver and gold with such passion, more than even Christ Himself is worshipped. Our living God is often scorned because of humanity's greed and reverence for that lifeless metal. Was there perhaps more religious madness in pagan rites? Do we put more trust in raging Hercules, murderous Mars, an adulterous and incestuous Jupiter, or treacherous Mercury? Even if what that greatest prophet says should be true: "All gods of the nations are demons."[9] This ought to be understood in the sense that men serve demons and are very similar to them, as an attentive reader will easily find to be true in the worshipers of those demons and in the writers of their histories.

Among our writers, however, there is no doubt of this, and especially in the works of Lactantius Firmianus,[10] who, in revealing the whole world of the gods and the foul hidden lairs of their crimes, embraces in his very profound discussion the whole range of their existence, who they were, what they did, what their customs were, what life, death, and burial they had, all in that book in which he began to keep track of the bases of the true faith. How I wish that he had been able to lend as much strength to my own words (to use Jerome's expression) as he has easily destroyed the words of others.[11]

What if people do not yet believe with abiding faith that Christ has come? Will a Messiah be awaited, or more truly will the coming Antichrist be awaited, who is to be resisted as an enemy rather than be obeyed as a master? The Messiah, our true master, has already come; He is Christ Himself. He descended in lowly garments from the lap of the Father, where "in the beginning was the Word, and the Word was with God, and God was the Word," through Whom obviously "all things were made." His divinity's majesty was meanwhile hidden, and "the Word became flesh and lived among us."[12]

So why do the Jews remain asleep? What deadly drowsiness has overcome the eyes and minds of these wretched people that they prefer to hope and to wait than to embrace that One through Whom they may be saved? For as Augustine says, "Why do they still wait for another Christ although they read that He has been prophesied and they see fulfilled what could not be fulfilled except through Christ Himself?"[13] It is clear thus far to devoted and religious minds that unless Jesus Christ, His birth from the Virgin, the events of His life, His death on the Cross, Resurrection, ascent into heaven, and return for judgment were understood in the words of the prophets, their words, although inspired by the Holy Spirit, would seem to be fables and meaningless dreams. Therefore, my brothers, clinging to this excellent Creator, Redeemer, and Savior Who is so familiar with us, let us not wait for any other except Him, Who is going to return for judgment. May we joyously and fearlessly see His second coming!

The Jews, however, depriving themselves of this present joy through ignorance and arrogance, torture themselves with a meaningless hope for the future and a very stupid expectation. Indeed, of all six ages none is longer than this one which is now being lived, whose beginning we date from the birth of Christ. So why do those crazy people wait for someone or other of their tribe to come? Long ago they were torn away from their own homes and dispersed through the whole world and saved only as a mockery of themselves and as a witness of Him, Jesus Christ, Whom they had crucified. Scattered after the Resurrection and worn down repeatedly by divine judgment, do they not understand nor want to understand that the words which they read in the Psalm sung by David has been fulfilled in them? "Bring me back to life, and I will seek retribution against them."[14]

Popular histories of the time testify to this; the overthrow of Jerusalem testifies to how great a ruin that city was. I do not even want to mention the awful starvation and the unbelievable, horrible crimes committed under the pretext of hunger, crimes which cannot be recounted here. The very number of those who died, because it exceeds all semblance of truth, serves as an indication and may be found in the works of the historians of that time, especially in the works of Josephus, a man of no ordinary authority who was present during that war.[15] Ought any pious person doubt that there was any other cause of all these evils but the nation's lack of faith and its ingratitude toward Christ? The beginning of all their ruin started with this incomprehensible and despicable waiting, which Christ Himself is said to have tearfully predicted as He took pity on that city which was doomed to perish, giving the reason that the city "had not recognized the time of its own calling,"[16] and this lack of necessary recognition was certainly the reason for their continued waiting.

The story which Suetonius Tranquillus, that most diligent writer of history, accurately recalls is not known to everyone, but it is not any less true for that. "Throughout the entire East there had become very wide-spread an old and steadfast opinion that it was fated that at that time people who came from Judea would gain control of the world."[17] As a non-Christian, however, he could by rights use the name of Fate, which we consider suspect. He predicted that the prophecy would be fulfilled with the elevation of Vespasian, who became emperor while waging war in Judea.[18] We, however, have to believe that it referred to the Messiah, which had already been fulfilled by the coming of Christ. As blind men do not see that which has been put before them, they kept on waiting for what had already passed, just as they wait today and will wait, we believe, until the end of time.

Then bolstered by that confidence, with the wisdom of God mocking them, how cruelly and irreverently they themselves had mocked Him and had impaled Him to the wood of the Cross. As if they were already the future masters of the world, they wanted to shake off the Roman yoke, killing the governor and putting to flight the imperial representa-tive in Syria, a rebellion which offered the Romans the inducement to move into the East and to besiege Jerusalem. This was done under the leadership of Vespasian, who led with him into war his firstborn son Titus, by whose advice and courage, but certainly with the approval of God (a thing which Titus himself is said to have admitted), the city was completely overthrown in the end and the race destroyed.[19]

However, that is certainly enough about the Jews.

What next? Should we listen to the cunning tales of Mohammed or the conflicting and undecipherable mysteries of philosophers and the filth of reckless Averroes and the poisoned cries and spewings passed from his foul mouth to heaven? Would we rather hear about him or listen to the sacrilegious statements of Photinus, or the ridiculous words of Manicheus, or the blasphemies of Arius?[20] If all these words are far from sound hearts, if neither the pitiful error of the pagans, nor the stiff-necked and obstinate blindness of the Jews, nor the hateful fury of the Saracens, nor the airy sophisms of fallacious philosophers, nor the devi-ant and exotic dogmas of heretics, touch or delight our minds or show us no hope whatsoever of salvation, for what do we search, for what do we live, or for what port do we head in the shipwreck of this life if it is not Christ? Anyone who has thrown the anchor of his hope on Him, even

when he is exposed to different gusts of persecutions, can indeed ride out
the waves and keep working; he can neither drown nor perish while
Christ is praying and at the same time ordering him "not to let your faith
fail you."[21]

But we must not listen to Christ's own enemy, who is also our enemy,
about Christ. Uninvited, Satan whispers many things about Him in our
minds, suggesting that Christ should not be believed and should be
scorned, although Satan himself, as it has been written, "both believes in
Him and trembles."[22]

Satan, however, has countless ways and hidden approaches for invad-
ing our souls. Often when he is cut off from one direction, he relies on
another. Most industrious of all, he leaves nothing untried, as ignorant
of how to rest after success as he is after defeat, so that it can quite appropriately be said of him what Hannibal said about Marcellus: "This is
doubtless the case when your enemy can bear neither good nor bad fortune: if he wins, he presses ferociously on the conquered; if he is defeated, he renews his battle against the victors."[23] Nor will Satan dare to
assert that anything is impossible for God lest he himself lose credibility
by such open perfidiousness.

Therefore what should we deduce? That God can do everything, that
He wishes furthermore to bestow all blessings on the human race, who
are weak and unworthy of His divine blessings? As a matter of fact, that
thought often disturbs many people's minds: certainly God is the best,
but I am the worst. Is there any proportion to such a discrepancy?

I know not only from the authority of our writers, but also from the
assertion of Plato, that envy has been banished as far away as possible
from Him Who is the best. On the other hand, I know that evil has been
bound to me as closely as possible. What difference does it make how
ready He may be to bless when I am not deserving of receiving His
blessing? I confess that the mercy of God is infinite, but I admit that I am
not fit for it, and the more my mind is limited and obsessed by my sins,
the greater His mercy is. Nothing is impossible for God[24]; all the impos-
sibility of rising up from so great a burden of sins is on me, and I am
overwhelmed. He is powerful enough to bestow salvation; I cannot be
saved. However great the mercy of God may be, certainly it does not
exclude justice. Although it may be immense, His mercy must be given
weight in proportion to my misery, for as the natural scientists say, the
actions of agents have no influence on anything unprepared to accept it.

Indeed, just as a tiny spark sets fire to dry stubble, so the force of water extinguishes the strong flame.

These thoughts, and other meditations like them, hover before our minds. Indeed, if they bring a healthy fear after shattering our sluggishness, we must value such unspoken advice as if it were the advice of angels who love us. If, however, they take away all our hope and trust, we should avoid hostile lies and precipitous roads to ruin, for where do they lead the souls who follow them if not to desperation, which is the worst of all evils?

Let nothing terrify us: God's power is not limited by any natural boundaries. Not only does it exercise its own power over those objects which are disposed, but it also disposes what has not been prepared. The mercy of God far transcends human misery and justice, and if it does not obliterate them, nevertheless it tempers and curbs them. As holy men have noted in David's words, not without reason does the Psalm writer, surrounding justice with a barrier of mercy on either side, say afterward: "Merciful and just is the Lord," and added "and our God finds mercy,"[25] as if he were not denying that God is just, but that the hands of justice are bound by the chains of mercy.

Is it not true that even as He will bring justice to an end in mercy, so someday He will bring mercy to an end in justice? Either "God will forget to take pity," as the same Psalmist says, "or He will hold back His mercy because of His anger."[26] Far be it from Him to do this; far be it from us to believe this. When a man decides that God does not wish to have mercy on those who repent and that His mercy is limited to the amount man himself sins, he is ignorant of God or fails to consider His power and mercy. However great the sin of mankind may be, it is certainly finite, but the goodness of God and His power are infinite. Therefore everything is safe with this lifesaving hope. When you cast away that hope, all is finished. Lacking a rudder, the ship of our soul is driven on the sea of this life by waves of events and winds of temptation. Nowhere is there a port where hope used to direct us nor a heaven which hope used to show us, but "the sea is on all sides," as Vergil says,[27] whence come shipwrecks and storms.

Let this, therefore, be the most important goal: Hold onto your hope; let nobody twist it away from you. Even if we hope for really great things, they are great things for us; there is nothing great for God, in Whose presence "our existence is as nothing,"[28] and before Whose eyes "a thousand years are like yesterday, which has passed away."²⁹ They are great, I confess, nay certainly immense, if they are compared to human merits. Lift up your minds to your Bestower: everything will seem small, not only possible, but also easy. What is there, I ask, which forces our hope to waver and our spirits to totter? We will seem to ourselves to be worthy of punishment and unworthy of mercy, nor are we mistaken in either case because it is our lot to be afflicted and His to have mercy. It is fitting that His worth should absorb our lack of worth, a phenomenon which certainly could not happen if mankind's sinfulness were able to impede God's mercy.

Although we merit His hatred, He is worthy of clemency and mercy. He is worthy to spare all. He is worthy to hate nothing of all the things that He has made. He is worthy not to lose any of all those people whom His Father has given over to Him. With all these things considered, because all the things done for humanity appear to be miraculous works of God and replete with ineffable grace, nothing will seem impossible, nothing incredible, because this fundamental point stands: God is omnipotent and good, with the result that nothing is able to be considered so great that He cannot do it, nothing so generous that He does not wish to do it. Based on these grounds, anything which faith has produced will stand solid and wholly intact when confronted by hostile sapping, battering rams, and whatever Satan will have erected. All of his attacks and power will be beaten back by ready and easy responses.

Everything is obvious when these things are welcomed in faith: we know that God, produced of virgin birth, has come among humanity and has lived among us, that He taught the path of life, was crucified, suffered, died, descended to hell, laid waste Tartarus, ascended to heaven, and is to come again in time. These are great achievements, I confess, but what one of all these is impossible for God?

If He has been able to do everything, which of all the things which He knows pertain to the salvation of His creation would He not wish to do? What has Christ, the son of God, the true God, not been able to accomplish which Isaiah, that unsullied servant of God, was not able to know and announce before it happened? Not only Isaiah or other prophets, but even the Sibyl, prophesied this so that every sex and every condition might testify to the coming of God. Isaiah says: "Lo! a virgin will conceive and will produce a son."³⁰ I wonder what the Jews think, what they are waiting for, when they read these words. They are ashamed, I think, to change their opinion, yet I proclaim to those wretched people with an unrestrained voice that this prophecy of Isaiah has been fulfilled in Mary, and never again will a virgin either conceive or give birth.

I pass over other holy prophecies of this sort and others about Christ, which are too time-consuming and unnecessary to add because there are too many of them and they are all too well-known to everyone. Let us listen, however, to what the Erithrean Sibyl predicted about Christ, even if she was speaking about Augustus Caesar, under whose reign Christ was going to be born from the Virgin, when she said, "Then a peace-making bull with a gentle lowing will bring the inhabited regions of the world under tributes." Look now how she agrees with the account of the evangelists, where it is handed down that "a decree went out from Caesar Augustus that a registration should be made for the whole world."[31] The same priestess at first dealt briefly with the coming of God in these words, saying, "In the days of this decree a heavenly lamb will come." Not much later she expands on this: "In the final age," she says, "God will be humbled, as will His divine offspring. Deity will be joined to humanity, a lamb will lie in the hay, and God and humanity will be brought up by the care of a maiden."[32] I do not understand how the evangelist who had seen events could have expressed them more clearly than did that prescient woman with the impulse of her inspired mind. She even prophesied the arrival of His forerunner John the Baptist, saying, "Signs will come first to those who believe: a very old woman will conceive a son who knows the future." Then she followed the course of His life and death thus, saying, "He will choose for Himself twelve in number from the fishermen and the down-trodden, one of whom will be a devil. Not by sword or war will He overthrow the city and kings of Aeneas' followers, but by the hook of a fisherman. By His lowly state and by poverty He will overcome wealth and crush pride. With His own death He will bring the dead back to life, and although He will be sacrificed, He will live and rule. All those things will come to pass, and there will be a regeneration. On the final day He will judge the good and the wicked."[33]

She then pursues many other topics, very similar to that found in the evangelists and in the Apostle Paul, and finally she also speaks of well-known rituals which have arisen in the church very recently. It is enough for me now to have touched upon those matters which pertain to the character of Christ Himself, all of which we see have been fulfilled in the very order in which they had been predicted, with the obvious exception of the Last Judgment, which we await, certain of its reality, but unsure about its time. For this analysis I have carefully extracted and included these prophecies, which are undoubtedly from the book of the Erithrean Sibyl, because they seemed not so well-recognized. Although writers disagree whether they belong to the Erithrean Sibyl or the Cumean Sibyl, there are, nevertheless, many other statements of the sort that their authoress seems to be counted among the citizens of the city of God.

It is clearly agreed that the words which follow were those of the Sibyl, even if it is unsure which one because Varro counts ten Sibyls, and he was the most serious and learned of the Latin writers.[34] They are words which Lactantius puts in various places in the first book of his *Divine Institutions,* but which Augustine, collecting them again in this order, includes in his eighteenth book of *The City of God.* Here he says, "He will later come into the hands of nonbelievers, who will box Him on the ears with impure hands, and from their foul mouths they will spit out poisoned venom, but to their lashings He will give His innocent and holy back. So that He may speak to the dead and be crowned with a wreath of thorns, He will remain quiet as He accepts their blows, lest someone acknowledge that He is the Word and its origin. For food they gave Him gall, and for thirst, vinegar. Such is the inhospitable table which they offered. Foolish race, you yourself have not understood your God, Who plays with the minds of mortals, but you have crowned Him with thorns and have provided Him with a foul, poisonous gall. The awning of your temple will be rent, and in the middle of the day there will be the darkest night for three hours. And He will die, and sleep will envelop Him for three days. Then, emerging from hell, He will be the first to come back to life, revived to show the beginning of the Resurrection."[35]

These are the prophecies of the Sibyl. Of whichever Sibyl they may be, they have been found to be ancient. If they were the words of the Erithrean Sibyl, who would doubt that they were by far the oldest? Indeed, although there are those who place her later during the rule of Romulus about the time of the founding of Rome, others report, however, that she prophesied long before in the time of the Trojan war. There seems to be no doubt that the Cumean Sibyl flourished at that time. If anyone should consider these prophecies diligently, they would seem no less evangelical than prophetic, that is, no less history than prophecy. Their very obvious clarity makes one think that they are speaking of past events, which is also the custom of prophets.

So that I may not have to prove this with any more citations, I will note that Gregory showed that one statement of the Sibyl was consistent with that of David when he said, "And they gave poison into my food, and in my thirst they have made me drunk on vinegar."[36] You have heard what she has said, certainly so similar that they seem to have been spoken by the same mouth, and beyond any shadow of a doubt, the two were speaking with the same inspiration. Indeed, these words and a thousand others had been spoken about Christ long before He was born in the flesh, and they were repeated about the very time of His birth in order to awaken humanity's faith in the true and eternal Son of God.

This happened not only through the prophets and His chosen people, but also through foreigners, whether they were holy like Job or even infidels not knowing what they were saying. For this purpose we can use the words which Vergil wrote when speaking about someone else in his *Bucolics*: "Even now a virgin returns, the Golden Age of Saturn returns. Now a new offspring is issued from lofty heaven."[37] Furthermore, writing in his *Aeneid* about the reign of Augustus, under whom we have said previously that Christ was born, he said, "In anticipation of his coming even now the Caspian kingdoms and the land of Maeotia shudder at the responses of the gods, and the frightened mouths of the seven-branched Nile are in distress."[38] Indeed, although these words were spoken about Caesar, the religious and devout reader will ascribe them to the heavenly King, Whose arrival had been preceded by signs all over the world. Hearing these portents and not aspiring any higher, the poet fixed on the arrival of the Roman emperor because he knew nothing greater than this, but had the true light shone into his eyes, he would doubtlessly have attributed the signs to the arrival of Another.

❧   ❧   ❧

NOTES

1. John 10:38.
2. Ps. 13:1.
3. Cf. Ps. 113:5-7, Ps. 134:16-17, Wisd. 15:15.
4. Isa. 40:18-20.
5. Horace, *Satires* 1.8.2-3.
6. Ps. 113:4, 134:15.
7. Ps. 113:9, 134:18.
8. Juvenal, *Satires* 1.113-14.
9. Ps. 95:5.
10. Lactantius Firmianus (fl. late 3rd century C.E.) was a Latin Church Father famous for his Ciceronian eloquence.
11. Jerome, *Epistles* 58.10.
12. John 1:1, 3, 14.
13. Augustine, *City of God* 28.35.
14. Ps. 40:11.
15. Flavius Josephus (c.37 C.E.–c.100 C.E.) was a Jewish historian. He authored *The Jewish War,* the history of the Roman-Jewish War of 66–70 C.E. Cf. *The Jewish War* 5.16.7.
16. Luke 19:44.
17. Suetonius, *Lives of the Caesars,* Vespasian 4. Suetonius Tranquillus (69–post 122 C.E.) wrote the *Lives of the Caesars* (Julius through Domitian).
18. Vespasian was the Emperor of Rome 69–79 C.E.
19. Titus, Vespasian's older son, had led the sack of Jerusalem in 70 C.E. and was emperor of Rome 79–81.
20. Photinus, bishop of Sirmo, was condemned as an Arian heretic by the Council of Antioch and died in 376. Arius, a theologian of Antioch (d. 336), was condemned as a heretic by the Council of Nicaea in 325 for his denial of the divinity of Christ. Mani (c.215–276/7) was a dualist, who believed in the existence of two gods, one of good and the other of evil, who are in eternal combat. He was the founder of Manichaeism.
21. Luke 22:32.
22. James 2:19.
23. Livy, *From the Founding of the City* 27.14.1. Hannibal (247–183 B.C.E.) was the Carthaginian general who led an invasion of Italy during the Second Punic

War. Marcellus, a Roman general, was a fierce opponent of Hannibal and seized Sicily from the Carthaginians in 212 B.C.E.

24. Cf. Matt. 19:26.

25. Ps. 114:5.

26. Ps. 76:10.

27. Vergil, *Aeneid* 3.193.

28. Ps. 38:6.

29. Ps. 89:4.

30. Isa. 7:14.

31. Luke 2:1.

32. *Book of the Erithrean Sibyl,* Codex Paris. 8500, fols. 51v-54v.

33. Petrarch, *On Human Affairs* 4.30.7.

34. Marcus Terentius Varro (116–23 B.C.E.) perhaps the greatest scholar of the late Republican period, wrote extensively on Roman religion.

35. Augustine, *City of God* 18.23. Cf. Lactantius, *Divine Institutions* 4.18.

36. Ps. 68:22.

37. Vergil, *Bucolics (Eclogues)* 4.6, 7.

38. Vergil, *Aeneid* 6.798, 800.

5

Even without citations from other sources, however, all these revelations are now clear to us, thanks to that One Who has loved us so much although we did not deserve it. The rays of His divine light pour into the eyes of the faithful in such a way that no one is so blind as not to perceive Christ in his mind as the "sunshine of righteousness."[1] Although the saying "Blessed are the eyes which see what you see"[2] may be the truest saying from the Truth itself, nevertheless I will demonstrate that in a certain sense there is little difference between our normal, corporeal sight and the clarity of this internal light by which devoted souls will see Christ, not with human eyes, but with a spiritual vision, now and until the end of time after Christ's Resurrection.

Indeed, I boldly confess (for who would deny it) that blessed are the eyes to which Christ appeared in the flesh. How sweet it would have been to see the sight of God dressed in our own flesh and our own soul's breath, to hear His words, to see His walk, to note His actions while He wandered among humanity, He Whom angels hold in awe, Whom they worship, by Whose glance they are fed, in Whose power they rejoice! Ah! to have been able to say of this grand and miraculous sight: Lo, this is a man Whom I hear, Whom I touch, Whom I see; a mortal man, I say, a real man, I say, Who lacks nothing of our humanness except sin and the stain of our humanity. And again: Lo, the same God, now inhabiting the earth and enduring earthly hardships, poverty, hunger, cold, heat, mental and physical pains; in the end He is going to suffer the cross, but dying on it, He is going to conquer death. Look how He Who created the heaven and the earth treads the earth with mortal feet, and "was born a man on earth and as the very Highest He founded it."[3] Just to see Him led to death, that One Who at the same time controlled the sun, the moon, and the stars by His power, to look at Him hanging on that fork-shaped yoke, weak, scarcely holding up His head, a man Who at that time fully ruled and supported the sky, lands, and the sea with His power to such an extent that not only did an earthquake shake the lands, but a shadowy pallor enshrouded the sky when the world was shaken at a nod of its Creator. How sweet it would have been to believe that all those events happened for our salvation. How great and enviable would such an opportunity as this have been for faithful souls!

Although we may be the lowest of mortal beings, there is, however, something even more fortunate which seems to have befallen us. Who now would be surprised that he is condemned for his friendship with Christ? Who would be reluctant to have the same thing happen to him as happened to Christ? He was indeed damned (amazingly enough) by many for having established the sacred friendship He did because He had been born and lived among those whom He could and wished to save. Many people deservedly said that this son of a carpenter, an eater of flesh, was possessed of demons, that He seduced people and blasphemed. Observing this, He Himself said, "No prophet is without honor except in his own land."[4]

Someone may point out, however, that He suffered these things at the hands of those who did not believe. I will admit that, but we have learned both that the faith of believers wavered and that even the very hearts of the Apostles were shaken by the death of the Savior, and we have read that Thomas' resistance to believing would benefit later generations. If these things could happen to the faithful with Christ alive or resurrected, why should we wonder that there are so many blasphemers against Christ when He has returned to heaven, whence He had come, and is removed from human sight? It was to these that our Fathers, especially Augustine, so eagerly and sagaciously responded that they convinced Porphyrius, that man of sharp intellect whose eyes were stunned by the pure light of truth.[5]

What should I say about that which people claim was spoken, not by the mouth of a man, but by the mouth of some god, as they call him, surely by the mouth of a demon? For when he saw that Christ's name, grief, and torment were being celebrated throughout the earth beyond any expectation, and that the true faith was constantly being strengthened by the tribulations of martyrs, he did not dare to deny what was obvious in the eyes of all and began to prophesy with strange and ambiguous words. Not daring at that time to speak against Christ, he said that the Apostle Peter had established the basis of the Christian faith with enchantments and magic arts, that it would last only three hundred and sixty years, and when those were completed, it would immediately collapse. I do not see what he wanted to gain for himself by that lie except that he simply could not give up his habit of lying, or (an explanation I am more inclined to believe) he wanted to create doubt in the souls of miserable people. Once those souls were turned away from the rays of the resurrected light, his aim was to call them back to the mists of the former darkness. Thus, because he despaired about the future, he would take what gain he could in the interim.

Everything has turned out contrary to his hope in this matter. There were more martyrs in that age than there have been subsequently in all generations or than we believe there will be up to the day of judgment. In the same way in which his silly and false spirit (whoever he might be) vindicates Christ, not by spontaneous love, but by forced reverence, so he makes Peter, a very innocent and simple fisherman, guilty of sorcery. With nothing to support his words, it is clearly false that Peter, who suffered tribulations, many dangers, and a cruel and ignominious death, sought fame for someone else by using magic arts, or that he zealously accomplished what we have already mentioned above so that Christ, not Peter himself, might be considered God in such a short time.

The question of Augustine seems to me to be the most penetrating here, for he says, "If Peter the magician caused the world to love Christ so much, what did the innocent Christ do to make Peter love Him?"[6] No less effective was the response he added: "So let those same people give themselves an answer, and if they can, let them understand that this happened by heavenly grace; that because of eternal life which He gave us, the world loves Christ, by Whose grace it was made; and that Peter loved Christ because of that eternal life which can be received only from Him and because Christ even suffered temporal death for his sake."[7]

It is less helpful for me to cite his remaining remarks than to marvel over these words: O noble soul, O divine force of genius, which lacks neither the light for exposing the deceit of enemies nor the strength for reinforcing the minds of friends, whose question and answer are worthy of a fighter for the faith and an athlete of the truth! Therefore, I consider it enough that the standard-bearer of *The City of God,* where he discusses these matters, often terrified the army of the enemy by his counsels and repulsed their impious attacks from his walls, both restoring and saving the peace of the Church. Augustine often demonstrated this ability elsewhere in his works, especially in that tirade against the foe when he destroyed the lie by which the devil seemed to reduce unending faith in Christ to such a narrow limit of time. By his reckoning of years Augustine taught that what Satan had predicted was false and that the predestined end of the duration of Christianity had already passed in his own time while he was writing that book and even that passage. If I consider correctly, moreover, thirty-five years after the time in which it was believed that the name of Christ would pass into utter disuse, idols were thrown down in the very name of Christ in Africa near Carthage. Thus, both the solid foundation of faith and the crowning glory of the Church were decorated by the spoils of the enemy while that enemy was especially hoping for the downfall of that same Church.

Firmly, piously, clearly, and faithfully Augustine laid hold of that sacrilege, as was his custom, and ferreted out the lie.[8] Otherwise, the proof could perhaps have seemed too insubstantial to souls slow in believing, with the devil suggesting that just because there had been a small mistake about the time, his prophecy did not seem for that reason utterly false.

This brings me back to what I was saying previously when I began to assert that we are more fortunate in our age [see page 46]. We have not seen Christ in the flesh the same way He appeared to His Apostles, although we may constantly see Him in the works of His miracles unless we close our eyes. Now, at least, we see a faith which has grown roots and has become strong, where our predecessors often saw it shaky. We see the worship of Christ spread far and wide, and although our laziness and folly do not reflect on Christ, but only on us, nevertheless the praise of Christ still resounds much more widely than it did then. We view with wonder empires and kings, formerly the persecutors of the Christian religion, now boasting in the name of Christ and in the ignominy of the Cross. We see country folk now surer about their faith than the Apostle Thomas was then: they seek neither His wounds nor the site of the nails. We know many people who have died for Christ without fear, who are ready to die for Him, and who are unmoved not only by the words of a servant girl tending the door of a house, but also by the threats and tortures of all tyrants.[9] We know that the madness of those who lack faith has been overcome by patience, that the hard-heartedness of butchers has been worn down, that shame has fallen upon the judges, and that martyrs have suddenly escaped from their executioners.

I shall not, however, compare us sinners to the Apostles or to their followers, nor shall I compare our age to that one, except for this reason: unless I am mistaken, I see that the gift of divine grace has come to us by the generous gift of Him "Who gives to everyone richly and does not cast reproach,"[10] and Who not only gives equal standing to those laboring in the eleventh hour and earlier, but also promotes to first place those who come last. In offering His divine rewards, He begins with them.[11]

Certainly Christ has kept His promise and fulfilled in us what He said to Thomas: "Because you have seen, you have believed. Blessed are whose who have not seen, yet have believed."[12]

Those people had the opportunity to see Christ in person; we have the chance to see a solid and universal faith in Christ, errors ground down by the heel, heresies beaten, and all misrepresentations made by wicked people or impure spirits torn out by the roots. We no longer see idols being overthrown, but we do see that just as souls have left bodies through death, so impious and evil spirits have abandoned idols through the power of our faith. Writers during that great period of our history confess this happened to the oracle of Apollo at Delphi in the earliest age of faith, although, being ignorant of the reason, they lament this as a most serious loss, boasting that "their age lacked no gift of the gods greater than the oracle at Delphi, a gift which has grown silent."[13] Lucan, you should, however, have known the cause of this. Indeed, you would not have complained, but would rather have congratulated yourself, because that crafty old Satan, whom Lactantius called the "Africanus of the gods,"[14] and who had used false persuasion to spread the word that he was the god of prophecy and more divine than all others, had grown speechless and confused by the arrival of Christ and feared to tell lies and deceive the world before the eyes of truth.

This has been happening from the beginning, as I have said. Later, however, demons were put to flight, a thing which church history and the deeds of the saints confirm, with those very demons shouting with a horrible wailing: "Jesus, son of the living God, why have You come to torture us before our time?"[15] As if He, Who had come before He was expected by them, that is, before the day of judgment, had come early. In the end temples were destroyed and statues overthrown until it reached the point that for some time neither temples of the gods nor idols remained to be broken or destroyed.

Therefore, I can say that the truest and fullest accomplishment of time has now and for some time arrived, about which a second demon seems to have whispered less spitefully, but without doubt more truly, to a certain follower and friend. For what else does that mournful complaint of Trimegistus to Asclepius mean?[16] If I may borrow a saying of Augustine for my own, "the grief of demons spoke"[17] through Trimegistus.

Trimegistus regards Egypt as the image of heaven and the temple of the whole world. I call it the source of all superstitions and errors, a place which could worship not only Isis and Osiris, but also bulls and that bloody animal the crocodile, and could adore those wanton creatures about which it would take me too long to speak. He laments the fact that Egypt will someday be deprived of its idols, as if there might be something better for humanity than to be freed from error and false opinion, or anything worse for humanity than that the miserable soul should serve the work of its own hands and that a person should tremble before his own creation. Indeed, he says that there will be a time when these things may happen which have now (thanks be to God!) actually happened, not only in Egypt, but in almost the whole world. Although Augustine says that this was accomplished in his own age, and he speaks the truth, nevertheless, because of the closeness of the predetermined time to the prophecy, some sort of doubt still troubled weak and lazy souls.

Now because not just one span, but a little less than four periods of three hundred and sixty-five years have passed with the faith of Christ always standing firm and over time increasing in many places, who does not understand that Satan lied when he ascribed this number of years to the life span of our religion and that he simply did not know what he was saying or wanted to deceive us?[18] Although it is as we have said, for many people this matter is still in doubt because there is such a fog of suspicion, such confusion of minds, and such sluggish diffidence. This is not because anyone completely doubts the power of God (unless he were out of his mind), but because a human being lacks faith in his own merits and does not dare to wish for or hope for as much as he sees given to him gratuitously. Comparing such a magnitude of heavenly blessings with his own lack of worth, he begins to doubt and to ask himself whether his blessings are real or a delusion, as if he were mocked by a blessed dream, as if there is a role for human merit in this life, and as if life were not totally the operation of the grace of God, not only that we are happy, but that we exist.

What I said above is therefore true indeed: it will seem to us that we are worthy, not of grace, but of punishment; nor indeed are we wrong. We are worthy of punishment: "We have sinned the same as our fathers; we have acted unjustly; we have done evil."[19] The same Psalmist, however, may cause us to ask whether our fathers with impunity forgot the works of God, scorned His counsel, tempted God, angered His friend Moses, made the images of calves, worshipped carved images, whispered in the tabernacles, ate the sacrifices of the dead, sacrificed their sons to demons, and poured forth innocent blood.[20] Although that Psalmist concluded with words of God's mercy, which in God are always infinite, unceasing, and steady, nevertheless, he says earlier, "The earth opened and swallowed Dathan and covered over the population of Abiram, a flame burst out in the synagogue and burnt the sinners, and God was irate in His fury toward His people and despised His heirs,"[21] that is, He turned away from them, for thus that passage is interpreted, and this abandonment is the worst evil and the closest to ultimate ruin.

❧ ❧ ❧

NOTES

1. Mal. 4:2. Cf. Petrarch, *Lyric Poems* 366.44.

2. Luke 10:23.

3. Ps. 86:5.

4. Matt. 13:57.

5. Porphyry (233–304 C.E.) was a Neo-Platonic philosopher.

6. Augustine, *City of God* 18.53.

7. Ibid.

8. Cf. Augustine, *City of God* 18.54.

9. In the immediate aftermath of the seizure of Christ by the authorities, Peter, when identified by a servant girl as a disciple of Christ, denied that he know Him (Matt. 26:67-70).

10. James 1:5.

11. Cf. Matt. 20:1-16.

12. John 20:29.

13. Lucan, *Pharsalia* 5.111-13.

14. Lactantius, *Divine Institutions* 1.9.

15. Matt. 8:29.

16. Cf. Hermes Trimegistus, *Asclepius* 24. The mystical writings appearing under the name of Hermes Trimegistus were composed in the 3rd century C.E. but were believed to have been written much earlier.

17. Augustine, *City of God* 8.26.

18. Note that earlier Christianity was predicted to endure 360 years, not 365 (see above, page 46).

19. Ps. 105:6.

20. Cf. Ps. 105 passim.

21. Ps. 105:17-18, 40. The son of Elich was in league with Dathan. They rebelled against Moses and were both swallowed up by the earth.

6

Do we perhaps go unpunished for no good reason? We are punished every day. There are threats on all sides, prods everywhere, whips around us; nevertheless, we neither stop nor tighten the reins on whatever desire captures our fancy. We do not suffer what we deserve to suffer, I confess, but we suffer many punishments which we would otherwise suffer only to a minimal extent if it were not for the penalty and punishment of sin.

Did those earliest ancestors undergo too small a punishment when the highest peaks of the mountains were covered by a universal flood? When the ancestors of the human race and of all other breathing things were saved by that huge ark, from which descended those creatures before whom the wide seas appeared and the receding waves offered the sight of a mountain track? Did they themselves go unpunished while God angrily rained down sulfurous and fiery balls of death from heaven onto impious civilizations?

Were the Egyptians punished too little when they were beset constantly by so many various plagues sent from heaven? Were the Assyrians punished too little while they were forced to serve effeminate kings? Were the Greeks punished too little when flourishing peoples and conquering states were divided against themselves? As Justinus says, "as long as they desired to rule individually, they all lost their power."[1] Those things happened with the arrival of the Macedonians, a nation until then unknown and obscure, but which would come to glory by the downfall of others. Were the Macedonians themselves punished too little when, after unexpectedly being exalted to the heavens, they suddenly fell to ruin and saw their kings being dragged in chains before the chariots of Roman generals to the Capitoline Hill?[2]

Were the Sicilians and Spaniards punished too little at the hands of the Romans and Carthaginians, like weak and defenseless sheep among ravenous wolves, for a long time the prey now of this army, now of that one? One final example: was Italy punished too little at the hands of the Romans, seeing so many outstanding and ancient neighbors oppressed in unforeseen servitude to that new race? All Italy itself, finally, was constantly worn down by the tumult and countless wars of five hundred years and was conquered without much resistance. Did Carthage itself and (to keep this short) all other nations and the whole world of evil suffer too little when in common indignation and grief the whole human race was forced under the yoke of one people? Was this because of the Roman people, who, as the historian Florus says, "in the two hundred years which follow" the five hundred about which we just spoke "were spreading through Africa, Europa, Asia, and in the end the whole world through wars and victories"?[3] How well did the Romans themselves, those conquerors of nations, act when in the very flower of their rising power their city was burned by the flames of the Senonian Gauls or after conquering the world with so much effort, they struggled so painfully with internal discord and used foreign victories as an impetus to civil war, turning their victorious weapons against themselves after everyone else had been conquered?[4]

Let me pass over those more recent barbarities: we see Italy, Africa, France, and Spain so often the plunder of Goths, Huns, Lombards, and Vandals. We see so many barbarian invasions, so many people slaughtered, the ruins of so many cities, and besides this before our eyes are the evils of our own age, which I cannot behold without tears. We see wars everywhere, an impassable sea infested with bandits, inhospitable lands, and nothing safe anywhere when treaties among humans are broken, nothing safe from violation, and where there had been a house of peace for a century[5] and the name of war unheard of by our ancestors, we now see bands of wandering plunderers, gloomy solitude, devastation, fear in all places, scarcely even sparing the very thresholds of Christ's church.

Add to this the grievous and tragic downfall of kings: one's neck was broken by a noose, another's body was cut short by a sword, the prison of another defiled by both sword and noose.[6] In what age had such things been heard to have happened at the same time? In what annals were they read? Nevertheless, we have seen all these things with our own eyes. Historians attest to the presence of such evil, and our seeing it somehow diminishes the wonder of hearing about it.[7] I speak of matters known to all peoples: the leaders of kingdoms, Naples, the greater Balearic Islands, and Paris attest to this.[8]

Add to this the plague, which without precedent is mowing down the whole mortal race from the rising to the setting of the sun as if it carried a sickle; add cities depleted of citizens, fields devoted to burials, now expanded places for tombs and bodies, and everywhere the pile of bodies lying about with no distinction of class or honor, and great tracts of land covered with vile ashes.

Add to this unusual earthquakes: the city of Rome, the head of the world, has been shaken, its towers pushed over, its churches laid low, a large part of Italy and the Alps themselves and the neighboring parts of Germany have trembled. The Rhine has felt it, as has that noble, half-Latin city which they call Basilea [Basel, Bale], which held the left bank of that river, crowning the solid heights of the bank which rises above the river. That city seemed inaccessible to chance misfortune if any place on land were safe. I saw this city last year: it seemed so much more an Italian city among barbarian cities that whether it was the propinquity of its lands or the innate amiability of its inhabitants, it made the full month's delay during which I waited there for the Holy Roman Emperor not only agreeable to me, but pleasant. In the end, since my waiting was in vain, I set out for a period of about twenty days to search out this prince. On my return, the appearance of that city had been turned in some strange and pathetic way into nothing.[9] Just a little while before, the magnificent appearance of its homes, the civilized character of its citizens, the leader of the city, an outstanding man, and my friends who had been my fellow students at Bologna when I was a boy and had now been restored to me after so many years — each of these things had delighted my mind and alleviated the tediousness of my wait. In a short while, however, nothing presented itself to me except mountains of rocks, silence, and the horror of those watching with their eyes and minds. So sudden was the change that one could only think that he was being mocked by some dream, that he had been or was now being deceived.

Add to these universal woes their evil effects on individual lives, grief, physical and mental afflictions, and dangers of a thousand sorts. Why would you not be afraid? Let me forget the things which people fear, a thousand forms of toil and the tedium of life, for nothing is more oppressive than these. Add to these thousands of temptations, the undying plots of demons, (and with the permission of all-powerful God) the violent attacks of spirits, and so many internal, never-ending battles for our souls. I cannot even begin to mention the evils appropriate for each age of mankind: the lack of seriousness during childhood, adolescent passions, the struggles of manhood, worry and gloom, restless cares and unresolved complaints (the companions of old age), and finally fear of death, unmercifully respecting neither glory nor power. At last think of all the common fears of mortals and, if I may use the name of fate in a religious discussion, that inexorable monster and "the roaring of greedy

55

Acheron,"[10] the disorder of the world and the stormy whirlpool of death. Anyone who has been able to "cast it beneath his feet"[11] is deservedly described as blessed by the poet, with whatever sort of blessedness there is to be hoped for in this vale of tears.

Let me touch upon a few of these issues out of the many. I am silent about our nakedness in which we are more miserable than any other creature. I pass over our frailty, which is not so obvious in any other creature. I will not mention mankind's neediness, which is not so destitute and abject in any other creature. I will not speak of our fruitless hopes, which are worrisome, unending, and insatiable. I am silent about our blind lust for life, the useless horror of death, grief that comes too soon, and laughter that comes too late, the very blindness of the soul's ignorance of itself, our ridiculous lack of knowledge of all sorts of matters, and our laborious quest for that knowledge which realizes more every day what it lacks and which, because of the increase of knowledge, accumulates more reasons for labor, grief, and unworthiness.

At this point I could bring up many such matters both public and private, but the preceding are sufficient and disturbing enough. If I should want to talk about them all, I would have to fill not just the chapter of one book, but many volumes. This is a task I think I will pursue in some other work insofar as I have strength and leisure.

More pertinent to this endeavor, however, are humanity's sins, which have created all the problems and the remaining plagues of the world, which are innumerable and limitless. If there were no sins, there would be no human misery, no disaster, no confusion, no death. Now, however, they are so great that they bring with them another evil even greater than the goads of our conscience: our fear of judgment and the ever-present punishments by which we are constantly chastened. This is above every other evil: our sins make us unfaithful, lacking in belief, continually desperate, and, as if God did not care for human concerns, prone to all crime and shame. So it seems to us that we are unable to imagine that such great heavenly benefits such as these are being conferred on us in return for our merits, as if God could not pity more than humanity can sin, and as if that verse of the prophet were not true: "When You will be angry, remember Your mercy,"[12] as well as other words which have been spoken previously about these matters.

The force of our conscience erases everything from our memory to such an extent that we daily stand in amazement that the world exists, unmindful of that which has been written: "The mercy of God is the reason that we have not been destroyed."[13] This mercy is certainly the invincible column and the immovable foundation which holds up a world weighed down by such a great collection of sins. Although He takes pity, He also punishes, and although He punishes the just more sparingly, nevertheless, He does so harshly. Let the man who does not believe that this is true look at himself. Anyone will find in his own home not only his own share of tribulations, a discovery which will prove that I have been speaking truly, but a bit more than he can bear.

There are a few exceptional people abounding in the things of this world. "They are not part of the hardship of humanity, nor will they be punished with humanity."[14] Nevertheless, if anyone should enter into the sanctuary of God, "let him consider what the final end of these people will be."[15] Alas! How much graver and more enduring punishments are reserved for them! Nor should anyone, seeing all these punishments, think that I diminish the mercy of God with my words. Rather, I prove that mercy has been mixed with justice.

I want especially to soften and destroy the hardness of certain people who, despite their many sins, dare not hope for mercy alone. Although He may punish as a judge, He takes pity as a father, retaining much more of a father's mercy than a judge's rigor. If it were not so and had He Who established human nature not helped cure it, for a long time now there would be nothing left for which we could be punished, so much greater is the force of the disease than the vigor of humanity, which lies sick and wounded. Who could explain in human words, or even conceive in the human mind, the magnitude of His grace or the height of His counsel for the sons of humanity? Truly we need divine assistance to measure God's gift, and it is by the grace of God that we recognize the grace of God. It is not for man to survey the celestial mystery on his own; nevertheless, because those who are both blind and lame, albeit wearied in the shadows, tremble as they seek the straight path, I shall speak a few words about these matters of which I seek knowledge more than I profess to know.

Look! Our weakness is always before our eyes. We do nothing that does not warn us of the human condition and its misery, about which some authors have published whole books, and still others distinguished treatises. Pliny the Elder touched on this briefly in the seventh book of his *Natural History*,[16] but in an excellent style and a flourishing abundance of ideas. Augustine wrote more broadly about this in his book *The City of God*.[17] Coming before all the others, Cicero dedicated his *Consolation* to this subject. I too have sometimes had the inspiration to write something and to cast my wandering pen into those realms, except that the matter seemed too great and too well known. So many different ideas would have offered themselves that I would be unsure where to begin or what would be the most important points to make. I thought that so great a matter could never be sufficiently explained and that whatever was said about the matter would seem redundant: nobody, I thought, could say anything new about it.

Therefore it is enough to have remembered this one thing: nothing is more miserable than humanity, nothing weaker, nothing poorer and more needy of outside assistance. Although we may have experienced such poverty, weakness, and misery, we know without books, without the admonition of anyone, where we are coming from, what we are, and what our future may be. Unless we are fooling ourselves, we know what paths we are taking, whence we are coming, and whither we are going. As long as we are mindful of ourselves, we cannot forget these matters.

To the contrary, however, we do not so much know the all-powerful majesty of divine nature as imagine it and contemplate it, "looking at the mysteries of God through those signs which we have come to understand."[18] Standing in awe, with the light of the sun overcoming our mortal eyes, we know this one thing, not that we know nothing, as Socrates says, who trusted his own intellect too little, but that we know this certainly: that this Being is unutterable, incomprehensible, and inaccessible to our minds. Horror and astonishment strike the mind of the person who contemplates both our own low estate and God's height at the same time. This is something we cannot even comprehend fully after it has happened. Who would have thought it before it happened? How powerful and merciful is this remedy which God has provided for our terrible misery! We who are blind and weak are still not able to bear the intensity of so much light, nor do we dare to fix our eyes on that Light which we love. Nevertheless, we are blessed by such weakness in that grace has been given to us. I do not say "more than we deserve" or "more than we ought to deserve." All our merit shriveled with our original parent Adam, just as the greenness of a tree dries up in its root. I do not say "more grace than we can repay by expressing appropriate gratitude toward Him at least in prayer," but "more grace than we can understand or dimly suspect."

Rejoice therefore, human nature, which has been made more blessed from its extreme misery than it would be able to conceive of with all its intelligence. Focus your educated geniuses on this, I ask. Listen, Plato, Aristotle, and Pythagoras: here lies hidden, not that ridiculous cycle and fanciful migration of souls, but a certain greater mystery of true salvation. Listen, Varro, most learned of humanity, you who searched most ardently after mysterious matters: here is described not the council of your gods and their fallacies, but the truth and worship of the one God.

Step forth, Cicero and Demosthenes. This is a heavenly, not a public, debate. See what your talent and ability can do here. You too, Homer and Vergil, be present in spirit: here are neither Greek kings nor Roman emperors nor generals nor Jupiter, that false "ruler of highest Olympus."[19] Christ, the true ruler of heaven, is being celebrated. Consider the great distance between heaven and earth, and when you have worked in vain for such a long time, I pray that you work profitably and imagine in your minds that for the earth to be saved, it must be joined to heaven. How will this happen? Here I require your cleverness and intelligence. I imagine you have never considered such matters. Come on, think and try hard, sharpen your minds, elevate your natural powers. Although your minds will soon have risen high, I think they will not reach this goal. Fatigued from the labor of their searching, they will fall back.

You have left for future generations many keenly treated and minutely investigated discussions about clouds, rain, lightning, winds, ice, snow, storms, hail, the nature of animals, the power of herbs, the properties of matter, many tracts as well about the swelling of the sea, the shaking of the lands, the movement of the sky and the stars, but from all those studies you have not seen how heaven was joined and united to the earth as one. It may seem great, perhaps, and certainly impossible and contrary to the laws of nature to join places which are so large and so distant, yet there is something greater and far more distant which has to be moved and bent for the world to be saved.

To be sure, I confess that the distance between heaven and earth is really huge, but it is finite, whereas between God and humanity the distance is infinite. Indeed, humanity is the earth, from which he has received his name.[20] Humanity has risen from the earth, lives on the earth, and is destined to return to the earth. God, however, is not heaven, but the Creator of heaven, as high from heaven as from earth, as much present and as much distant in both places. If we should concede that heaven is finer than earth, the creator and ruler of both would nevertheless still be that same God "Who made heaven and earth, the seas and everything which is in them,"[21] and because He does not fill a particular space, He rules justly and towers over all His creation.

So what will happen? I ask you, most learned men, who have entrusted to your books and to memory many matters with more curiosity than necessary, but have been silent about the one thing that is the greatest, most salutary, and essential. It is known, and Augustine testifies to this, that some of your manuscripts prophesied God and contain His Word and many matters which agree with the writings of the Evangelists that concern the highest matters of faith and the Son Who abides together with His Father forever. These words, "In the beginning was the Word, and the Word was with God, and God was the Word,"[22] and "all things were made through Him and without Him nothing was made,"[23] and these words, "the Word was made flesh," and how it was joined to earth and "lived among us,"[24] "these things learned Plato did not know," says Jerome, and "eloquent Demosthenes was ignorant of them."[25] The former of these writers is reported to have said, "No God is mixed with humans."[26] You, however, Plato, either said this falsely, or the odiousness associated with this opinion was falsely directed against you.

How much better in this regard was Seneca, for he said "God will come to humanity; no mind is good without God."[27] Surely our God has come to us so that we might go to Him, and that same God of ours interacted with humanity when He lived among us, "showing himself like a man in appearance."[28] There is certainly one thing which Plato, denying it, did not know, and which Seneca did not know either, although he admitted it. This was a thing quite unknown to humanity, unless His divinity had revealed it to someone (and that has been in accordance with the fixed law of the divine plan from the beginning of time), that is, that humanity had to be raised up, and divinity brought down. Each happened equally, and this is the celebrated union without which humanity would have lain sick and languishing forever. Neither one could have happened without the other, nor could it have happened in any other way through some other force than through Him Who "bent His heavens and descended,"[29] Who looks at the earth and makes it tremble. Through Him, therefore, and not through another did this happen.

What an indescribable sacrament! To what higher end was humanity able to be raised than that a human being, consisting of a rational soul and human flesh, a human being, exposed to our mortal accidents, dangers, and needs, in brief, a true and perfect man, inexplicably assumed into one person with the Word, the Son of God, consubstantial with the Father and co-eternal with Him. To what higher end was humanity able to be raised than that this perfect man would join two natures in Himself by a wondrous union of totally disparate elements? To what higher end, I say, could a human being ascend than that a person could be God? On the other hand, how could divinity be lowered and reduced more than when it assumed a mortal body which would suffer persecution, insults, terrors, and all of our evils except sin, and then suffered the ultimate abuse: whippings, passion, and "a death on the cross."[30] Humbled, He descended for the salvation of humanity, which He had raised.

❧   ❧   ❧

NOTES

1. Justin 8.1.1. The *Epitome* of Justin (3rd century C.E.) was a summary of the the *Philippic Histories* of Pompeius Trogus, who flourished in the age of Augustus.

2. After the defeat of Perseus, king of Macedon, by the Romans in 168 B.C.E., the king and his sons were forced to march in the triumphal procession at Rome of their conqueror Lucius Aemilius Paulus.

3. Florus 1.18, 2.1. Anneus Florus (2nd century C.E.) wrote a brief history of Rome down to the time of Augustus.

4. The Senonian Gauls burned Rome in 390 B.C.E. Rome experienced several civil wars from the struggle between Marius and Sulla in 88 B.C.E. to the victory of Octavian over Anthony and Cleopatra in 31 B.C.E.

5. Petrarch suggests here that for a century France has not suffered a major war.

6. Cf. Petrarch, *Remedies for Fortune Fair and Foul*, Preface 4.

7. Cf. Petrarch, *Remedies* 1.88, 2.91; Seneca, *Epistles* 10.2.

8. Cf. Petrarch, *Remedies* 2.92. Petrarch is referring to the murder of Andrew of Hungary, reputedly by his wife, Joanna of Naples, in 1345; the death of King Jaime of Majorca in battle in 1349; and the capture of John II, king of France, by the English in 1356.

9. Petrarch is referring to the earthquake that destroyed Basel in 1356.

10. Vergil, *Georgics* 2.492.

11. Ibid.

12. Hab. 3:2.

13. Lam. 3:22.

14. Ps. 72:5.

15. Deut. 32:20.

16. Pliny, *Natural History* 7.6. See also p. 135 n. 28. Pliny the Elder (23–79 C.E.) was a Roman scentific writer.

17. Augustine, *City of God* 22.22.

18. Rom. 1:20.

19. Vergil, *Aeneid* 2.779.

20. Petrarch makes a false etymological connection between the Latin word *humanus* (human), whose root is *homo* (person), and *humus* (ground, earth).

21. Ps. 145:6, Acts 14:14.

22. John 1:1.

23. John 1:3.

24. John 1:14.

25. Jerome, *Epistles* 53.4.

26. Ibid.

27. Seneca, *Epistles* 73.16.

28. Phil. 2:7.

29. Ps. 17:10.

30. Phil. 2:8.

7

Mortal minds have created for themselves countless heresies concerning matters which are grasped, not by intelligence at least, but only by faith, and which so far surpass understanding that mortal intelligence, stubborn and proud, cannot grasp them. There are two such heresies in particular. One states that Christ was only God and not a human being, the other contends that He was only a human being and not God.[1] Moreover, the stubbornness of each of these heresies, similar to the stubbornness of the rest of them, bruised by the hammers of the true faith, offers a warning to the faithful, but eternal ruin to their proponents. By now the Truth has been spread so far that that fatal doctrine's poison can no longer deceive or hide undetected. Our eyes and our hands perceive everything everywhere. In vain does an heretical quack appear at the doors of the faithful. The foe, invisible in vain, is surrounded. All his guiles lie visible; all his wiles are transparent. Even a rough shepherd will scorn him, as will the iron-clad soldier, the hardy ditch-digger, the unsleeping merchant, the wandering sailor, even the faithful old grandmother, for even if people do not know their articles of faith and its defense exactly, their pious ears, which have grown accustomed to true doctrines and have been filled with the sound of divine and heavenly thunderclaps, are protected against all sacrilege both by the simplicity of confession and by the strength of faith.

However, when the enemy has been overcome and driven away by the strength of faith, he will seek other ploys. He will play upon the toil of work, the fruitlessness of time, and its unlikely success. He will say, "All right, let Christ be God. Who will obey Him? Who will carry out such harsh orders? If God wanted humanity to be saved, He would have given them either more strength or lighter orders." Again: who has figured out God's plan when even the plans of humans are concealed from other people? Who knows, therefore, whether He commands in order to arouse us or whether He threatens so that on the Day of Judgment He will recollect what commands have been fulfilled and forget those that have been neglected.

My brothers, let us all protest this wicked and falsely spoken suggestion. Let us all cry out to God. He will hear us, and our righteous clamor will ring in His ears.[2] Let each of us say this with all our soul. If we can, let each of us sprinkle his voice with tears and break his voice with sighs.

No melody is more pleasing to God. He wants to be loved; He wants people to hope in Him; He wants to be invoked with lamentations.

However, let each person say, "Lord, free my soul from wicked lips and from a deceitful tongue."[3] The spirit of evil does not have flesh and bones, nor does it have a tongue and a voice. So how does it speak? O how I wish there were no weapons and that our perils could be helped by its disarming! Maybe this does not happen because the more laboriously our army fights against this enemy, the more visible and acceptable it is to God our leader. Within our soul our enemy the devil says many things which we all must resist silently and after long training. We must fortify ourselves and be on guard against such enemies and their well-known schemes. They are enemies whom we experience inside our walls, as I have said, and even in the innermost recesses of our soul.

Moreover, spirits sometimes do have both a tongue and a voice. Someone may say, "What tongues do you mean?" To be sure, the tongues of wicked people, the voice of the mob, if indeed out of so many tongues the entire population has one voice. That voice praises desire, despises virtue, and says that the road of Christ is either inaccessible or at least uncertain. Truth has few witnesses. We live in this situation. We have been cast into this little block of time. I say we ought not to take advantage of these practices, but resist them. I say this is hard work and quite difficult for us miserable people, who are still on a voyage of doubtful outcome amidst the waves of this age. We are constantly drawn in by the tide of worldly attractions. Only an interruption of our sins and preoccupations gives us any respite.

You, on the other hand, who have already reached the port of that uncertain voyage, have a safe vantage point and a much easier chance to provide for the future. Indeed, you have cut away the knots of the world, the nooses of business, the chains of normal affairs. Unencumbered and free, you have survived many storms, and now you are where you take rest and time. Therefore, blessed with the required free time for that extraordinary contemplation of salvation which alone has been the goal of your struggle, neglecting all other concerns, frugally, soberly, and watchfully take advantage of this great gift of God, albeit understood only by a few, lest out of your leisure, as happens, some more upsetting preoccupation may arise for you. Indeed, you do not need a leisure which is relaxed and indolent and which weakens your minds, but one which is strong and, especially in view of your unique character, religious and dutiful.

Therefore, my brothers, do this; continue along this path to salvation. No other path is straighter, none is safer, and for this reason I have asked you so often today to take time.

Where Jerome's translation of the Bible says, "Take time,"[4] an older translation said "Manage your free time." Augustine adheres to the latter when he says: "We certainly seek one thing, than which nothing is simpler. So let us seek it with simplicity of heart. Manage your free time, he says, and you will realize that I am God. This is not a leisure of idleness, but a leisure of thought that should be free from limits of place and time."[5] What profound and wonderful advice, my brothers, is that which he added so it would be clearly understood: "For these fantasies of pride and mutability do not allow us to see the enduring oneness. Limits of place offer us something to love; limits of time take away what we love and leave in our minds crowds of illusions by which our desire is aroused to one thing or another. Thus our minds become disquieted and reproachful, hoping in vain to attain those things which attract it. The mind, therefore, is called to leisure with the result that it may not desire those things which cannot be desired without effort."[6] That man who was great for both his devotion and his writings said this.

My brothers, I call you to this leisure, I demand this, I encourage this, I beg this: manage your leisure and take time. These two counsels are the best; nay, they are the same thing as are the words that follow: "You will realize that I am God" and "you will see that I am God."[7] The way is sweet; the end blessed. Taking time to see, to manage leisure, to realize, and to climb, not only with minimal effort to eternal rest, a goal which itself is highly desirable, but also through worldly joy to eternal blessings, will grant you the reward of immense grace. Climb to this summit, from where there is a way of ascending even higher, and stop on the peak of this leisure. Here, with no noise muffling your hearing, with no dust of passing distractions to block your eyes, behold all the guiles and snares of the enemy. Even though, as I have said (thanks be to Christ, Who has taught us the whole truth), we have reached the point where well-trained minds and ears, whether by their own nature or by habit that has become nature, have learned to reject anything which by the very words themselves sounds opposed to the truth, nevertheless we must beware that more subtle, devilish murmur of the impious one (whose appearance may seem better, but whose reality is worse) who may think that by praising Christ he is impeding that journey of yours by which you reach Christ. He will certainly act this way; he may say, "I confess that whatever Christ orders is holy, but to fulfill the commands of God is more than humanity can do. Therefore, if in the pursuit of human affairs we work to that point where we recognize, as often happens, that we are unequal to our undertaking, and on better counsel we stop, what should we hope for in our holy undertaking? So let us leave those matters to the angels, even the best of whom have crumbled under the weight. Let heavenly beings care for heavenly matters, and let us take care of human matters. Maybe we will make a better decision by not entering upon this steep and rugged journey rather than stopping in the middle of the path. Maybe it is better to enjoy this life while it is here than to lose what is certain by hoping for what is uncertain."

A second tempter will come — the closer he gets, the more dangerous he is — who will admit both that the pathways of Christ are right and that His commands are holy, who will not deny that these pathways are passable and these commands possible, but he will exaggerate the difficulty of our problems and weaknesses, especially that of our age, about whose hopeless and ruined ways nobody can say too much. He will scatter a chill of despair on our fervent purpose or, proclaiming perhaps that God's commands are easy, will conclude that we can wait to fulfill them. We should give part of our time to this life, to the pleasures to which youth is obviously more receptive; all the rest should be put off until feeble old age, which may be fit for more mature advice. Then, when the end of this life is near, we should think seriously about the life to come, especially because there should be a very natural sequence in all things, and having once put earlier pleasures away, the return to them is distasteful. People who have shown repentance have pleased God no less than those who have lived in such a way that they do not need this remedy.

There will be no lack of advocates of these and similar notions, either in other people's conversations or our own private thoughts. Who should be amazed at the effect of this when it affected Augustine, a fact which is well-known from his *Confessions*. It had also previously affected Anthony, a man of such rugged determination and of solid virtue and faith, a fact that is known from the testimony of Athanasius, who said, "The enemy of the Christian name, the devil, bearing with impatience so much virtue in his youth, attacked him with his old deceits and, at first trying to tempt him, if he could in some way pull him down from his besieged stance, sent to him the memory of his possessions, the need to protect his sister, the nobility of his family, the love of objects, the inconstant glory of the world, the various pleasures of food, and other enticements of the life he had left behind; finally he suggested the difficult goal of virtue and the enormous effort necessary to reach it, as well as the frailty of the body and the great length of time needed. Wishing to recall him from the right way, he aroused in him a great mist of thoughts."[8] So spoke Athanasius.

You, however, my brothers, repel these weapons of the enemy with the same shield of prayer which St. Anthony used, if indeed the weapon of the devil is whatever the mouth of the wicked says. So he casts many weapons because he has many tongues, as if he had as many slings with which he could hurl poison darts. He has not only tongues, but also eyes, ears, hands, arms, and feet. In a word, just as the soul of a just person is the abode of Christ, so the soul of the wicked is the abode of the devil, and just as the body obeys the soul, so the soul obeys the spirit which controls it.

So from this point, when Satan gives such persuasive arguments, what response can we make? What opposition can we set before that deceitful tongue? If you ask this, you will be answered by the prophet: "Sharp arrows of an All-powerful God, together with coals of desolation."[9] What an opportune and effective remedy for great evil! Elsewhere the same prophet says: "Just as arrows are in the hand of the powerful, so are the sons of the oppressed."[10] Not without reason someone usually asks: Who is this all-powerful God? What are these arrows? What are these coals? Certainly there is nobody all-powerful except that One to Whom this was said: "I know that You can accomplish everything and that no thought escapes You,"[11] and by another writer: "That You alone could do so much was always beyond my comprehension, and who will resist the strength of Your arm? Because the world is before You like a grain of cereal on a scale and like a drop of morning dew which rests on the earth, You have mercy on all people, for You can do everything."[12] Even more from another: "You are all-powerful, Lord, and Your truth is within Your compass."[13] And from another: "King of kings and Lord of lords, You alone are blessed and all-powerful, Who alone have immortality and live in a light which no man can approach."[14] And still another: "He crossed mountains, and these people whom He has overturned in His wrath do not know it. He rattles the earth from its place, and its columns tremble. He commands the sun, and the sun does not rise. He seals off the light. He extends the heavens and walks above the waves of the sea. He makes Arcturus, Orion, the Pleiades, and the constellations of the south. He makes countless great and inexplicable miracles."[15]

He is therefore, brothers, alone and truly all-powerful, for who else, I ask, is all-powerful, or how little is this power of ours? How great is our frailty in this narrow corner of the habitable world or (to speak appropriately) in this pinpoint of the habitable world, for if the earth is a pinpoint in relationship to the universe, this region is a pinpoint of a pinpoint. We mortals, a hard-working, fearful, and worried race, live in this pinpoint, which is weighed down by a great sea and by many swamps, inhospitable and uncultivated because of so many deserts, divided by so many streams and mountains, fragmented by so many kingdoms and empires, and upset by so many wars and uprisings. We pride ourselves in possessing this world, even with its continual problems, long labor, and for such a fleeting time, as if it will endure forever. Its blessings are ephemeral, even though with some strange gleam striking our eyes it may seem to be something else. We know what it really is through many experiences, but through none more clearly than through death.

What else could arrows mean except the Apostles and their messages, which that all-powerful God about Whom we speak cast into the midst of His enemy. The words of life and the testimony of the Gospel have been spread far and wide, either by the Apostles or by God Himself. God's word has pierced the chests of kings and populations with a wound which causes, not intense pain, but sweet love. About these arrows the Psalmist himself wrote, glorying and exulting, not once, but again and again: "Because I have avenged myself on them in the name of the Lord."[16] He is truly all-powerful Who has tamed the world with a few arrows, and having avenged Himself on so many of His adversaries, has rescued countless souls from the leader of our enemy (Satan). His arrows are truly sharp if with an easy throw they can fix themselves in the hardest heart.

What else does the Psalmist mean by the coals of desolation, or destroyers — for each term can be read in the ancient texts — than the ignited and burning souls which have preceded you in this holy endeavor? Often when words do not help, examples do. Although a person is not embarrassed to disbelieve someone's words, he is embarrassed not to imitate someone's example; so much weightier is the sting of examples than the sting of words. So against a deceitful tongue, lest it pierce a tender heart with its double prong, we have been offered these two remedies: the sharp arrows of the All-powerful and, if by chance they may not be enough, the coals of desolation.

❧   ❧   ❧

NOTES

1. At the Council of Nicaea (325 C.E.) the orthodox position became that Christ had both a human and a divine nature. Arius' position, which maintained that He had only a divine nature, was condemned as heretical.
2. Cf. Ps. 4:4, 90:15.
3. Ps. 119:2.
4. Ps. 45:11.
5. Augustine, *Of True Religion* 35.65.
6. Ibid.
7. Ps. 45:11.
8. Athanasius, *Life of St. Anthony* 4. See also PL 73.129b.
9. Ps. 119:4. Petrarch further explains "coals of desolation" on page 73.
10. Ps. 126:4.
11. Job 42:2.
12. Wisd. 11:22-24.
13. Ps. 88:9.
14. 1 Tim. 6:15-16.
15. Job 9:5-10.
16. Ps. 117:10-12.

8

Let me say something else so my argument will not lack examples. Because a deceitful tongue clamors around you, whoever you are in this life, you should meditate especially on how all-powerful God is, He Who has inspired you. How easy it is for Him to advance what He has inspired and to complete what He has begun. You hear a tongue mixing lies with Truth so that all the falsehoods will not be equally rejected. That tongue will say, "fear no one, submit yourself to no one. Nothing is better than freedom, so be free." Why are you dispirited by empty terror or by lowly slavery?

God will reply first with the voice of Moses, and the living Truth itself will say that "you should worship the Lord your God and serve Him alone."[1] Another friend of God will say, "Fear the Lord and serve Him with a heart that is perfect and most true."[2] And still another: "Remove foreign gods from your midst, prepare your hearts for the Lord, and serve Him alone."[3] The same writer again says, "Do not retreat, but serve God in all your heart and do not turn aside for useless things that will not benefit you."[4] Still another writer will say, "Serve the God of your fathers, and the wrath of His fury will turn away from you."[5] Not just men, but even a widow addressing God said, "All Your creation should serve You."[6] That prophetic King David, moreover, told both kings and all creation to serve the Lord, Who was to be served now in joy and now in fear.[7] Therefore I will serve Him in joy and in fear, and in this way I will be free. No, that is insufficient; by serving Him I will rule.

Satan will say, "Servitude is rough, the yoke is heavy." You will reply, "My Lord, Who is as truthful as you are mendacious, shouts to the contrary that 'His yoke is pleasant and His burden light.'"[8]

Satan will say, "You are a fragile, mortal sinner." Give this response: "My God is holy, brave, and immortal. If I should be exhausted, I will cling to Him and will rest in His lap. My fatigue both has its own pleasure and makes rest more pleasing." There are those who seek fatigue by exercising. To be sure, if anything oppresses me, I will go to Him. He is immovable, firm, and untiring. He loves me. He will not turn away so that I may be destroyed, but if I confide in Him, I will not be ashamed, nor will my friends laugh at me.

You will turn then to His divine counsel and arm yourself with the words of Christ Himself. Hear foretold by Him the problems, toils, dangers, and scandals of this life. Hear foretold by Him whatever you have to endure in the course of your existence. Obversely, hear about the rewards of a better life and the solace which is promised to those who work toward this goal. This is given to you and arms you against Satan's deceitful tongue.

If not even this is enough, if an even sharper spear of Satan continues to prod you and to emphasize your numerous sins and the frailty of your condition, that there is a hard road, a rough time, a huge burden, that you are spoiled, sensitive, weak, sickly, young, or old, remember that all these are the whisperings of his deceitful tongue. He will ask, "Why are you working? Where are you headed? Why are you so busy so early? Why do you stay at work so late? Rejoice while you can. Your fortune will look out for the future."

As often as you are beset by those arguments, my brothers, if neither words nor sharp arrows are sufficient for your defense, then you must call to mind those coals of desolation. Am I any weaker than women and girls, who often eagerly endured, not some minor labor as I have, but many terrible tortures and final punishment in the name of Christ? Am I more feeble than Gregory,[9] more fastidious than Arsenius,[10] more full of desire, and prouder than kings and their sons who so often have spurned their kingdoms, the pleasures of dominion, and even life itself for Christ?

You are neither the first nor the last to make this journey. Even you have leaders for your undertaking, for as Jerome said, "Each undertaking has its own leaders: let Roman leaders imitate the Camillans, the Fabricians, the Regulans, the Scipios; let philosophers model themselves after Pythagoras, Socrates, Plato, Aristotle; let the poets emulate Homer, Vergil, Menander, Terence; the historians: Thucydides, Sallust, Herodotus, Livy; orators: Lysias, the Gracchi brothers, Demosthenes, Cicero; and in our own age, let the bishops and elders have as their example the Apostles and their followers, whose honor and merit they should strive to possess in equal measure. We, however, have Paul, St. Anthony, Julian, Hilarion, and Macarius[11] as leaders of our undertaking, and so that we may return to the truth of the Scriptures, our leaders are Elijah and Elisha, our guides are the sons of the prophets."[12] Indeed, these are your leaders, who were Jerome's leaders.

Furthermore, Jerome, Augustine, Gregory, and just about anyone down to this day who has lived a solitary and reclusive life for love of Christ, are all your leaders and companions, supporters and helpers. They offer themselves as examples to follow as a kind of staff when you are burdened or tired from your journey. For this reason, if someone is young, you must call to mind Paul the hermit, Anthony, and Hilarion, the first of whom went into solitude and left the world when he was sixteen, the second at twenty or thereabouts, and the third at only fifteen. If anyone is too old, those same men should be kept before your eyes, their perseverance should especially be valued, and the end of their life should be linked to its beginning, for of the three, Paul reached his one hundred and thirteenth year, Anthony his hundred and fifth, and Hilarion his eightieth year in that fervor of holy and religious leisure.

It is not my intention to name others here, for I have mentioned them in the second half of my *Life of Solitude.* Therefore, let each person select from this group or another a leader whom he feels to be most suitable for him, and dwelling upon the examples of that leader's life, let him go forward with this leader in the footsteps of our King. If anyone by chance loses faith that he can be like that chosen leader, and if it seems difficult to imitate the ancient men who were unconquered in the wars of Christ, does it not occur to him that they were boys before they were old men? Furthermore, will you not be able to do what girls, invalids, and those raised to rule can do? As if these, however strong or weak they were, could do anything by themselves without the grace of that One Who comforted them and with Whose help the Apostle gloried that "he could do everything."[13]

Will old age draw us back from that virtue to which old age alone can drive us, when the traveler has begun to think that he is close to the end of the day, that the way is short and steeply down-sloping, with a resting place nearby and a reward prepared with an end to his labors? Did old age cause Victorinus to fear death after he rejected everything, especially his renown as a writer, for which he had become so widely known for such a long time, and after he renounced the honor of public office for the sake of Christ, Whom he either had not previously known or perhaps had held in contempt? He had been a pagan as a youth and as an old man, but a Christian in his old age. He was a blessed man who with easy payment corrected the mistakes of his long journey in the evening of his life![14]

Will the weight of conscience drive a person to desperation or oppress him as he remembers how many blessings David forgot and how many crimes he committed? Did he not attain mercy by not despairing? What a great persecutor of Christ was Paul? What great persecutions did he direct because of Christ? How great an enemy of the true faith was Augustine? How great a proponent of the same faith did he become? What about Mary Magdalene, "a woman, a sinner in the city,"[15] not in the city of God, I say, which sinners do not inhabit, but in the city of the world? Was she not changed from a citizen of Babylon into a citizen of the heavenly Jerusalem? Was she not so reformed through God's grace that, with the stains of her shamelessness wiped away, she seemed to us to have been first among maidens after the mother of Christ alone? It is a clear argument that although virginity itself may be irretrievable, nevertheless with penitence and tears the glory of virginity can be repaired, and very truly has this been said: he who has been forgiven the greater debt is the more beloved.[16]

These, therefore, are the burning coals. Whoever will use them as a defense will have peace. If anything horrid and perverse should fall to the depths of one's soul, whether taken there by the force of one's own tongue, by earthly cares, or by any recollection of one's own past vanity (none of which could happen without the sneaky or overt suggestions of that deceitful tongue), all such afflictions will be immediately destroyed by the coals of desolation and by holy fire. Thus by timely and therapeutic burning the human spirit is restored. Just as weeds grow in abundance when fertile soil has not been cultivated, a field of one's soul is cleansed and restored by timely and fruitful farming when it receives the nourishing seeds of the word of God.

To be sure, there may be those who, rushing too quickly though this passage in the psalm, want the arrows of the powerful — no, the truly all-powerful — to be received as the sentences of divine words; they want the coals of desolation to be received as the fire of the Holy Spirit, by which learned holy men sharpen their arrows.

They say that unless human preaching is kindled by a divine gust, it will be weak and useless for penetrating the listener's soul, whose heart has long been hardened by frost. Although some may accept this interpretation, the other is more useful and beyond any shadow of a doubt more productive. According to this latter interpretation, "all-powerful" means "Christ"; "arrows" means "His messages and words"; and "coals" mean "His examples." About this let nobody have any doubt. So that you may have more trust in this interpretation, no matter how I have expressed it, I confess that it has been excerpted in large part from the words of the saints, and from Augustine before all others.

Do not think that this is all you have to heed: there are countless matters against which you must always keep an armed and focused mind. Generally speaking, whatever unreasonable idea you consider in silence or hear from another comes from that deceitful tongue. Avoid his guiles, stay away from his treacheries. Be vigilant, for his speech and thought is covered by a brilliant veneer of reasoning. It has occurred to some, a thing which often happens even to great men, to ask for a sign, not from the foe, but from God. Beware: this is the counsel of the enemy. Satan does not dare to ask a well-ordered mind to seek a sign from himself lest his treachery be too obvious. He knows that there is not much confidence in him because of his habit of lying, so he persuades us to seek a sign from God, advice which implies loss of faith and merits disdain, for it is nothing more than an offense against God.

Do not consider this, my brothers. We are not among those to whom it has been said: "An evil and adulterous generation seeks a sign, and that sign will not be given to it."[17] Our adversary hopes that we will not learn. Our ignorance is most pleasing to him; our knowledge disturbs him. Rather Satan hopes that we will be confounded as he himself was when he heard from the Lord: "Go back, Satan; for it has been written that you will not tempt the Lord your God."[18] He does not want us to believe in our Lord, from Whom and through Whom and in Whom we exist, without some token; instead, he wants us, who have acquired a thousand such tokens, to demand new tokens which have no meaning, but will harm us, nevertheless, so that we may vex God with empty superstitions, thereby "hardening our hearts, just as during their tribulation after a second day of temptation in the desert, when our ancestors tempted Him, tested Him, and saw His works."[19] The foe suggests this to us as if we have forgotten how severely our ancestors were punished. He urges us who are fearful for the future to seek the present, which for mankind is neither possible, necessary, nor useful. Even if it were possible, it is a subject which I do not pursue lest I take too long, especially because such matters are treated elegantly by Cicero in that book which he wrote *On Divination*, and after him by Favorinus, a philosopher of great wit and learning.[20] Satan, however, wants us to be slaves of augurs, soothsayers, or those divining by any art which serves this purpose. Nevertheless, despising all these things is very easy for those who reflect upon this

Scripture: "It is a great affliction of humanity, which does not know the past and cannot know the future by any sign,"[21] and in the same book: "everything is kept uncertain in the future,"[22] and likewise, "humanity does not know what has happened before it; who will be able to show it what is going to happen after it?"[23]

Along the same lines as that writer, Statius said, "It is wrong for humanity to know what tomorrow's age will bring."[24] About all these sentiments I commend to you that saying of Accius: "Not one whit," he said, "do I trust augurs, who fill other people's ears with their words so that they may stock their own homes with gold."[25] No less does the mockery of Pacuvius please me, for he said, "If they foresee those things which are destined to happen, they are compared to Jupiter."[26] At this point, if the testimony of poets is not enough, hear the prophecy of Isaiah, who said, "Declare those things which are destined to happen in the future, and we will know that you are gods."[27]

This, however, is a fallacy sufficiently well-known to learned men and constitutes a danger for no one now except for the ignorant common crowd. Satan often secretly whispers that rash and headlong suggestion to us, that is, that we should hope for someone to rise again from the dead, from whom we might learn the reality of the other life and the truth of the Last Judgment, as if there might be some person who will wickedly come to life and say words truer than God does, Who lives for eternity, or His heralds, the Apostles and prophets, or as if we would more readily believe such a person. The Gospel has responded to this deceit when it says, "Indeed they have Moses and the prophets; let the people listen to them,"[28] and immediately thereafter, "If they do not listen to Moses and the prophets, they will not believe anyone risen from the dead."[29]

Nevertheless, Satan struggles in every way to make us desire with our damnable curiosity to see this or some other signs, miracles, or prodigies that we have read about and therefore believe are the basis of our faith. As I have said, however, this is the longing of an unbelieving and impatient soul which seeks a reason for rebellion. If we believe only those things which we see, no one will see the immortal and invisible God, or indeed any spirits, or his own soul, or at length anything eternal because, as it has been written, "the things which are not seen are eternal."[30]

If, however, anyone desires miracles to happen again so that he may believe them, with equal audacity he should demand the whole story of the Gospels to be repeated. So it will not suffice that Christ did anything once for our salvation, nor even twice or four times, because by some hereditary right of madness posterity is going to ask that what we have seen be repeated in every age. Nothing more unsuitable or more unfaithful than this can be imagined. Indeed, there must be a difference between knowledge and faith. Certainly, however, since faith comes from hearing, this desire reduces faith to an object of sight and touch so that it becomes experience, not faith. O Brothers, a faithful and devoted soul does not demand this, nor even consider it. Let it be enough for us to look through the eyes of the Apostles and the saints for our beliefs. We believe, but they know.

What other sort of good news did John announce when he said this? "He who has seen has presented his testimony, and his testimony is true. He knows that he speaks the truth so that even you may believe."[31] Whatever is sought beyond this is unnecessary, nay rather, is superstitious, if indeed as Pope Leo clearly said, "Through those men we were warned against the subterfuges of ignorant men and the arguments of worldly wisdom. Their sight has taught us; our listening to them has made us wiser; their touch has strengthened us. Let us, therefore, give thanks for divine guidance and the necessary caution of our holy fathers. They had their doubts so that we would have none."[32]

Although these words of Leo have become common knowledge, I said them because it is my intention now to write what is true and effective, not elegant and new. Let the wounds of martyrs and the holy blood flowing from them be enough for us. From this source our faith has been inscribed on pious minds. Martyrs would never have hurried so fearlessly and so happily to punishment and death if they had not received a suitable promise. Therefore, that I may add the well-known words of another, albeit minor, bishop: "We have learned that we argue at our own great peril about the truth of religion, which we see confirmed by the blood of so many people. It is a matter of great danger if after the oracles of the prophets, after the testimony of the Apostles, after the wounds of martyrs, you should presume to discuss the old faith as if it were a novelty, and if after such obvious guides you should remain in error, and after the sweat of the dying you should wrangle in a leisurely debate. Let us revere our faith in the glory of the sacred martyrs."[33] So spoke Maximus.[34]

From all these things, my brothers, the faithful ought to be persuaded that these blustery and frivolous arguments are intended to seek the favor of the common crowd, not the truth of Christ. All the empty quests for knowledge beyond our understanding and especially all the desire for miracles are a sign of obstinacy and curiosity, not of faith. To guard against this temptation, do not forget that saying of Augustine: "Those miracles have not been allowed to endure into our times," he said, "for this reason: so the mind would not always seek what is visible and the human race would not grow hardened from familiarity with those things by the novelty of which it once was passionately sought."[35]

Yes, he really said "grow hardened," nor would he be any more surprised by people's being brought back to life daily than he is surprised by people's being born daily, for how much greater it is to create what was not than to bring back to life what had been. Nevertheless, since we are moved more by things of less importance, the mother of wonder is rarity.

Certainly that same Augustine examined this argument more fully, replying to foes of the faith in another more familiar place, for he spoke thus: "Why, they say, do those miracles not happen now which you say have happened?"[36] In answer he said, "I could say that they were necessary before the world would believe, and for this reason, that the world would believe. Whoever still seeks prodigies so that he may believe is himself a great prodigy who does not believe when the whole world believes."[37] Striking out at the disease of hesitation, he said, "They say this, however, with the result that those miracles are not believed to have happened."[38] I want you, my brothers, to fasten your mind attentively to this point: all those people who demand miracles, whose ridiculous requests and urgings disgust us, are not so much greedy for the present or the future as they are incredulous of the past. By hoping and doubting less openly, but not less unfaithfully, they condemn their faith, which they do not dare to condemn by denial.

Nevertheless, whether or not miracles have occurred in our age, let us recognize the highest and only Bestower of miracles, and all the more let us thank Him Who has so stabilized our faith that we now believe without miracles. To be sure, by his sacred inspiration Augustine put to flight these ambiguities and these suspicions, which try to block the calm face of truth with clouds, for in that same place he said with no interruption, "So why is Christ elevated to heaven in the flesh on all sides in song with so much faith?"[39] Then using a Ciceronian phrase, as he often does for the defense of our belief, he says, "When these educated times reject everything that is impossible, why in the absence of any miracles does the world so amazingly believe the unbelievable? Will these things perhaps be said to have been believable and thus to have been believed? Why, therefore, do they themselves not believe?"⁴⁰ Coming to the end with great force, as is his custom, he said, "Our conclusion is short: either some unbelievable things, which nevertheless happened and were seen, created faith in some unbelievable thing which was not seen, or a thing believable in itself, such that it needed no miracles to persuade others, refuted the excessive faithlessness of those critics of the Faith."⁴¹

Because that is the way matters are, I say we certainly ought to abstain from the fellowship of demons. Indeed, it is the well-known punishment of a lying man that he is not believed when he speaks the truth. Therefore, what should happen to the fellow in whom there is no truth? The secure route is to avoid him: he who trusts a liar not one whit will not be fooled by a lie. So take time: nothing is better.

❧ ❧ ❧

NOTES

1. Deut. 6:13, 10:20; Matt. 4:10.

2. Jon. 24:14.

3. 1 Kings 7:3.

4. 1 Kings 12:20-21.

5. 2 Para. 30:8.

6. Judith 16:17.

7. Cf. Ps. 2:11, 71:11, 99:2.

8. Matt. 11:30.

9. Gregory the Great, bishop of Rome (540–604 C.E.), was one of the most important of medieval popes and a prolific writer.

10. Arsenius (d. 445 C.E.), member of a Roman senatorial family, was the tutor of the children of Emperor Theodosius at Constantinople.

11. Paul of Thebes (d. 341 C.E.), Julianus Saba (d. 377), Hilarion (d. 371), and Macarius (4th century) were all hermits.

12. Jerome, *Epistles* 57.5.

13. Phil. 4:13.

14. Cf. Augustine, *Confessions* 8.2. The conversion to Christianity of Marius Victorinus (mid-4th century), a famous orator and Neo-Platonist, made a deep impression on his own generation.

15. Luke 7:37.

16. Cf. Luke 7:42-43.

17. Matt. 12:39.

18. Matt. 4:10, 7.

19. Ps. 94:8-9.

20. Favorinus of Arles was a rhetorician at the court of the Roman Emperor Antonius Pius, who ruled 138–161 C.E.

21. Eccles. 8:6-7.

22. Eccles. 9:2.

23. Eccles. 10:14.

24. Statius, *Thebaid* 3.562-63; also Horace, *Odes* 1.11. Publius Papinius Statius (45–96 C.E.) wrote epics and other occasional poems.

25. Aulus Gellius, *Attic Nights* 14.1.34. Lucius Accius (2nd century B.C.E.) was a writer of Latin drama, festivals, and tragedies.

26. Aulus Gellius, *Attic Nights* 14.1.34. Marcus Pacuvius (220–c.130 B.C.E.) wrote Latin tragedies. Cicero considered him Rome's greatest tragic poet.

27. Isa. 41:23.

28. Luke 16:29.

29. Luke 16:31.

30. 2 Cor. 4:18; cf. Augustine, *Of True Religion* 3.3.

31. John 19:35.

32. Leo I, the Great, *Sermons* 73.1. Pope Leo I, who served 440–461, was one of the ablest of the early Roman popes. See also PL 54.395.

33. Leo I, the Great, *Sermons* 88.

34. Maximus, *Sermons* 88. Maximus was bishop of Turin c.420. This passage is found in PL 57.707.

35. Augustine, *Of True Religion* 25.47.

36. Augustine, *City of God* 22.8.

37. Ibid.

38. Ibid.

39. Ibid.

40. Ibid.

41. Ibid.

BOOK II

HERE BEGINS THE SECOND BOOK
ON RELIGIOUS LEISURE
BY THAT MOST ILLUSTRIOUS POET
FRANCESCO PETRARCH

I

In spite of our limitations, I believe we have now fought well enough under the leadership of Christ against the outrages of our greater enemy. We must continue to use that same guidance to strike down other enemies as well, the foremost of which is this world, whose brow is as enticing and whose looks as appealing as its ends are cruel and its secrets are foul. There is nothing real in its appearance, for it fulfills not one iota of all it promises. I think that we must free ourselves from its deceit and all earthly pretensions. Although these attractions may be numberless, they share one common purpose: to fool us by staying just beyond our grasp.

You have lived in the secular world. All of you, or as I suppose some of you, have experienced its enticing ways and know how absolutely nothing in it is solid or reliable, yet its wily tongue entices with meaningless words and passes itself off as something great, as if to deceive our forgetful souls or erase our memory. Certainly most of humanity's actions are concerned with worldly objects; if I were to mention each one, there would be enough material for me to write yet another volume.

All existence returns to nothingness, yet how mad and blind can we be! With what eagerness we amass riches which will perish, and how great is our concern for personal property which will neither last nor follow us! Meanwhile, we neglect that virtuousness which will accompany us to our death and carry us to heaven. Nothing is truer than this saying, which you ought to give in response to those passions and impulses of your spirit: "O vanity of vanities! All is vanity."[1] And this: "I have seen all that is done under the sun, and behold, all is vanity and an affliction of the spirit."[2] And likewise: "I have said in my heart that I will proceed to revel in my delights and enjoy my blessings. I have seen that this too was vanity."[3]

I will not mention the rest of the world's spoils and its empty boasting about its riches. The sum of it all is this: "Whatever my eyes have desired, I have refused them nothing. Nor did I keep my heart from enjoying every pleasure and from amusing itself with the things which I had done, and I considered it my due share that I should profit from my work."[4] Thus spoke Solomon, who was famous for his government and his great reputation for wisdom.

Many of his words fit you, my brothers, in spite of the fact that you are different from him in may ways. Let each one of you say on his own behalf: I too have thought and done such things, for I was not born a monk. I have come from the world; I have experienced Babylon. You cannot fool me, World, for I have tasted of you, I know you, and moreover, I have the example of a great leader before me. I have not been a king like Solomon, nor have I surpassed with my deeds all those who lived before my time in Jerusalem, as he did, yet I have been one of those busy men who both live and hope in you, the world. And what comes of it? At the end of all this, I trust in my own experience and not in you, for when I had awakened, and like Solomon "when I had turned to all the things which my hands had made and to that work over which I had sweated in vain, I saw in all of them vanity and a vexation of the spirit, and that nothing under the sun endures."[5] I omit other verses, for they are worn out by popular usage, nor do I have any intention of copying out Ecclesiastes.

So what is the point of all this? "I have grown tired of my life, seeing that all things under the sun are evil, that all are vanity and vexation of the spirit. Again, I have grown to hate all my effort, all those things for which I had struggled so eagerly beneath the sun because I would have an heir after me. I do not know whether he will be wise or foolish, yet he will be master of all that for which I have sweated and worried. Is there anything so vain as this? Whereupon I stopped, and my heart refused to toil any further under the sun."[6]

What Solomon says here ("he will be master") has been spoken even more bitterly by another in Ecclesiasticus: "He who hoards things unfairly for his own purpose piles up acquisitions for other men, and someone else will enjoy his blessings."[7]

The lyric poet Horace in his book of *Odes* spoke similarly of the enjoyments of one's heir with these verses: "Your more worthy heir will consume those fine Caecuban wines which you have stashed behind a hundred locks, and he will stain the floor[8] with that grand old vintage, although it may be more fit for the dinners of high priests."[9]

The satirist Juvenal, addressing this idea and arguing bitterly that greed is adverse and burdensome for oneself while it serves the pleasures of one's heir, says that it is undoubtedly folly and patently madness "to live the life of a beggar so that you may die rich."[10]

But I return to the uncertainty about an heir. Solomon says that he does not know whether his heir will be wise or foolish. Unless I am very wrong, this is really a minor complaint because no man knows either how wise or foolish his heir may be or whether his successor will be a friend, whoever his successor may be. Everywhere we see enemies becoming one's heirs. Among mortal fortunes there is scarcely any curse worse than this, and it is a problem unique to the wealthy.

Solomon spoke plainly about his doubts for his own heir. From whom else did he learn them than from his father, for David said in Psalm 37 [sic]: "All things are vanity; every man is mortal. Indeed, man goes about like a shadow, but he troubles himself in vain. So he gathers riches without knowing for whom he will amass them."[11] Again in Psalm 48 he says: "They will leave behind their wealth for someone else."[12] Here indeed, to make open mockery of the worries of rich men, which are no more beneficial than the ashes of one's tomb and the inconstancy of public favor, he added: "Their tombs will be their homes forever and their shelters from generation to generation even though they have given their names to their lands."[13]

Look! We have heard about the brevity of mortal fame: tombs for homes, the memory of posterity, and whatever other fame there may be for what is doomed to die. Given that all possessions are full of needless trouble and madness, that same Psalm advances a biting attack on brutish folly: "Man did not understand when he was honored; he has made himself like the beasts and has became similar to them."[14] Lest anyone hope that this foolishness may escape punishment, not only in this world but also in the next, look what he adds at this point: "Just like sheep they have been put to death, and death will feed upon them."[15]

Consequently, my brothers, all of one mind in Christ, throw any sharp arrows of this sort back at the deceptively flattering world. It does not take much effort. You know your present status and recall what you have left behind. You need no warning from me or anyone else, unless you value face-paint and shiny baubles more than the substance of things: those things are completely alien to the living force of noble intelligence. No palace can be compared to your cells. No glory can be compared to your humble state. No authority can be compared to your yoke. No sinful license can be compared to your innocence. No ostentation of worldly objects (no matter how elaborate) can be compared to your free time. No feasts can be compared to your fasting. Finally no purple finery can be compared to your sack cloth.

So leave others to rejoice in their purple robes, marble palaces, fleeting power, empty honors, pleasant amusements, and all the other trappings over which the citizens of Babylon gloat. For you, who are making your way to the eternal Jerusalem, "let there be no wish to rejoice in anything except the Cross of our Lord Jesus Christ, through Whom the world has been crucified for you, and you for the world."[16]

So now, scorn the world even if it entices you. Do not trust it. It is a liar, following the example of its own prince. As that eloquent man Claudian so aptly said, "The world is modeled after the example of its king."[17] Nor is it important to ask who this leader might be. Indeed, who is he other than the one whom our own Christ, the King of kings and Lord of lords, calls the "prince of this world," not once but again and again?

But if ever this same world, whose outer appearance is lovely, as I have said, tries to prevail somehow upon your senses (with which Satan has a great familiarity) while your reason is asleep, you should rouse your reason, curb those senses, and cry out from the earth, invoking heavenly protection. Cry all together and individually, "Save me, God, for the waters have come in all the way up to my soul."[18]

If this is the cry from our leader to our Father, it is fitting because we know that pleasures and carnal desires, which are unstable like water, are referred to by the name "waters." For what, I ask you, is more like flowing water than the endlessly changing affairs of human beings? Where are the fleeting, empty joys of all those who have devoted themselves to filthy pleasures and useless struggles from the beginning of the world to the present day? Just as those distractions have slipped away and turned into nothing, so will present joys and those who love them. They will slip away even more quickly than I write. As the Psalmist says, "They will arrive at nothing, just like running water," and "Like the wax that flows, they will be borne away."[19]

These are the rivers of Babylon which the Scriptures recount. Decay, instability, and the flight of all worldly things look to the ways of Babylon, not to that regal city whose inhabitants' "feet are standing within your halls, O Jerusalem."[20] For what else is Babylon except confusion itself? What is more confused than this world? Who is more confused than those who love it?

Would I be saying anything new if I were to note that those tales of hell may be applied quite literally to such people? I could be wrong, but isn't it true? The condition of human beings, the ebb and flow of life, and all aspects of existence are such that they seem to have been immersed in all the rivers of Tartarus and to have received some characteristic from each one. To have drunk deeply from the Lethe, one is overcome by forgetfulness of one's better nature; from the Phlegethon, the heat of anger and desire; from the Acheron, fruitless penitence and grief; from the Cocytus, lamentation and weeping; and from the Styx, enmity and hatred.[21] As a result, their evil ways never lack punishment. Indeed, the thirst of Tantalus will always torment them.[22] The crag of the Lapiths will terrify them. The rock of Sisyphus will wear them out. The vulture of Tityus will gnaw on them. The revolving wheel of Ixion will keep them spinning.

As others have written, I ask about whom you think this was rightly said? "The wicked walk in a circle of hell."[23] On whom would you say this next curse fell? "My God, put them before the face of the wind like a wheel and like chaff, like a fire which consumes a forest and like a flame which sets the mountains ablaze."[24] And no less this curse? "Let their paths be shadows and treachery."[25] There is nothing in all these citations except futile circles of scheming, flames of desires, discordant opinions, and inconstancy, all of which render life troubled and confused.

How else should I understand the River of Babylon than as the expression of how things do not, as we have carefully observed, endure? For such is the nature of a river: it both flees and stays at the same time. Although the waters flee, the river remains. Indeed, that is what Heraclitus meant to say when he said, "We step into the same river twice and yet we do not,"[26] and since he delighted in so much obscure speech, he was consequently given the name "the mysterious." Expanding on this, Seneca said, "The name of the river stays the same, but the waters have passed by."[27]

For example, let anyone step into this river on whose bank I am writing to you now.[28] Here at its source and its uppermost falls, it is a vigorous and quickly-flowing stream. Then, having stepped out, let him soon step back into it once again. It is the same river, the same stretch of bank, but the waters are different. What does it matter to these waters? Were they endowed with feeling? The river remains the same while its water is swept away?

How much more helpful is it to a mortal that the earth stays steady while he changes, although not even it remains the same (if we would speak the truth), rather it moves on, granted more subtly, toward its own end? It is also to our benefit that the cities in which we are born and raised endure a longer time, although we see even them grow old and die. Let no city hope for immortality because we see that Rome, the chief among our own cities, is mortal.

So that I may please the boys and novices among you who will read these words, I cite Prosper, who so elegantly says, "What good does it do me that rivers are carried along ever onward in their long course, their waters undepleted."[29] With numerous other words he arrives at this conclusion: "These rivers remain, but our ancestors have not remained. I live my life as a guest for a limited period of time."[30]

As I would also hope to please those of somewhat more advanced years, I note that Seneca said the very same thing, following closely that remark of Heraclitus[31] mentioned above: "In a river it is more obvious than in a man, but nevertheless a swift stream carries us, too, ever onward."[32] A greater observation occurs to me, I confess. A swifter and more obvious stream lays hold of mankind, for although the waters of a river flee, its appearance is the same. However, as the years of a man's life slip away, his appearance is so different and so altered that after a short time he cannot be recognized, even by friends and kin. Thus, as boyhood obscures infancy, and adolescence obscures boyhood, and adulthood, which the naturalists falsely call permanent, obscures both, at length, old age removes all other ages in the same way.

So it happens that, if contact is interrupted, in a brief time a friend may become unrecognizable. If Dardanus should return to Troy, or Romulus to Rome, after thousands of years, without any hesitation Dardanus would recognize the Xanthus River, Romulus the Tiber.[33] The change of humanity is so much more obvious than the passing of a river; therefore I fully endorse what Seneca said: "Therefore I really wonder at our loss of reason because we love something as fleeting as a body so much."[34]

Therefore, if a Gentile, who expected the loss of his body to be irreparable and had various doubts about the immortality of the soul, dared to say this, what can we, who are sure about our corruptible and perishable body and the future status of our soul, rightly say? If we use the body chastely and soberly, can we expect eternal incorruptibility and bliss? To be sure, if we have any concern for immortality, if we have any interest in a more blessed existence, we must despise this short period of corruption so that we may come to that eternal incorruptibility with great faith.

Now imagine the cities which you have inhabited, but do not long for them. A man who longs for storms when he is safe in port is out of his mind. Rejoice because you have escaped unscathed in your safe skiff from so great a shipwreck. The memory of your past tribulations is certainly pleasant, but longing for them is insane. Consider what these cities were like when you dwelt among the residents of "Babylon," for they all remind us of that city for the most part. You used to wander through the streets and walkways of those cities. You did not intend to pray in the temples, nor were you eager to sell in the market, but you were occupied with the sights. You wished to see and be seen and please the eyes of those people who had no direction, and did not care about the all-seeing eyes of the eternal Spectator.

Now imagine yourselves returning to those same cities. I ask, what do you suspect? Perhaps you will see well-known towers again and recognize ancient walls, although even they may soon fall to ruin. The places endure; the rivers flow by; the mountains stand. Hunt for the people you once knew. I do not know how it happens, but almost all of them will have disappeared. A great stupor will seize you as you enter that same city which has become yet another, and you may agree with Heraclitus, who said that we enter into the same city twice, but we do not enter it. I am still imprisoned in the chains of a sinner in the world, so when I look at old cities I have known, I seem to recognize them, but upon entering them, I find that I do not recognize them.

Cross the street and stand before the palaces of kings and priests and before the homes of proud citizens whom you once knew well. Maybe the walls still resist decay, but what of the inhabitants themselves? Knock on the doors, call out for them. If they are not home, wait a little until they return. How frightening does the saying of that simple and upright man seem, who said amidst his afflictions, "Wood has hope. If it is cut down, it will flourish again, and its branches will sprout. If its root grows old in the ground and its trunk dies in the dust, at the smell of water it will germinate and produce foliage just as when it was first planted."[35]

Do we hope that perhaps our condition may be the same? Alas! How dissimilar it is! These words follow next: "But when a human being dies, naked and wasted away, where is he, I ask?"[36] Let those who love this age tell us: where are their fathers? If they be silent, let Job himself answer: "In the same way, if the waters should recede from the sea and if the river, emptied of water, should dry up, thus humanity will not rise again once it has gone to sleep."[37] Still, lest he cut off hope of the resurrection with these words, he finally added: "Until heaven may be worn away, he will neither awaken nor rise from his sleep."[38]

Meanwhile, my brothers, the inhabitants of this earthly dwelling shall pass away and shall not return. Therefore, passing by favorite taverns, ask about friends whom you have left there. The raised eyebrow of an unknown customer will meet you on the threshold, horror will stand your hair on end, and your voice will stick in your throat when you hear that fortune has played games with their wealth and that death has done the same in its own way with mortals. Then that saying of Job in the metaphor of water may again strike you again: "My brothers have gone before me like a torrent which passes hurriedly in the valleys."[39] Believe me, for I know: once beloved cities will inspire you to hate and dread them. Everything has changed so much. Nothing of what had been so pleasing remains.

I might ask the ancients, Julius Caesar, Augustus, Tiberius, Gaius Caligula, Nero, Vespasian, Titus, Domitian, Trajan, Hadrian, and all the Antonines, whose names have been so beloved and so celebrated for so long in Rome and throughout the whole empire, to consider the fate of their cities. I might also ask Severus, Diocletian, Constantine, Valentinian, Theodosius, and the families who grew up to expect the sceptre! Examples that we see, however, touch our mind more effectively, and I do not want to recount ancient histories lest, because you are eager for silence, I waste your time with a narrative that is too long. I have diligently reported these ancient events in that book entitled *On Human Affairs*.[40] So consider a few instances which are more familiar to you. Where now is Boniface VIII, the Roman Pope and true wonder of the world, whom, unless I am mistaken, some of you saw? Where are his successors, John, Benedict, and the two Clements whom we indubitably saw?[41] Where is Henry, the emperor of the Holy Roman Empire?[42] Where is the French King Philip, who acquired the nickname "The Fair" after an untimely death stole him away just as it did his sons, who like their father were very attractive and succeeded him in turn? Their deaths were so untimely that the lives of all of them seemed to have been a dream. Where is that other Philip, the father of the present king, more fortunate than his son because he resides in a tomb, while a prison holds his son?[43] Where is the king of Spain who recently brought terror to the Saracens?[44] He was the shield of faith but is now subjected to attacks from the west. Finally, where is the glory of the Gauls and that crown of Italy, the Sicilian King Robert?[45] The storm of troubles following his death shows how fortunate you were to serve the eternal King during the time of his reign.

So that I may not speak too much longer, I shall pass over the majority of rulers and important kings. If you ask where these princes reside now, you will be shown tiny tombs decorated by the talent of minor artists. In death their sparkling tombs, adorned with jewels and gold, reflect their ambition in life. Representations of the dead live in Parian marble in accordance with that saying of that foremost poet: "They will produce living countenances from marble."[46] But I ask you: where are they themselves? Their titles and inscriptions are magnificent and their inscriptions are lofty-sounding, but empty. You stand astounded when you read them. But wait, I beg you, until the doorstep of that last resting place is opened, and new miracles and a new wonder appear. Alas! How small the amount of ash or how huge the amount of vermin and serpents there will be! What an unexpected transformation! How different is the face of reality! Where now are those armed companions? Where now are those groups of girls? Where now is Ganymede, who was summoned to be the cupbearer of the gods? Where now are the master chefs and the skilled carvers of fattened birds? Where now are the regal tapestries on the walls, the red carpet lying under foot, the ivory inlaid in wood, and the horny-hoofed horses champing at their golden reins? Where now is that ornate furniture, the Corinthian vases, the work of the artists of Damascus, and the animals etched on golden vases? Where now are the homes inlaid with cypress and ebony, the dining rooms, and the painted panels? Where now are the spectacles, songs, and banquets ferreted from the bowels of the earth and sea? Where are the wines which come from distant lands? Where are all the many enticements for lusts, the fine garments to cover the dirt on one's body, a head radiating with a crown, a stomach girded with a glowing sword belt, and index fingers dazzling with the spoils of the Indian shore and the talent of craftsmen? To finish this, where is the domineering wife? Where are the "sons like new plantations and the daughters decorated like unto a temple,"[47] who recently with enticing touches and sweet kisses soothed the neck of their dying father? What a sad and unhappy change! Everything has turned into worms and serpents. Everything eventually turns into nothingness.

Of course, unless I am wrong, this will have been a more productive vision and contemplation of the soul than that which Cicero recounts in his second book *On the Laws,* where he says that Athens is delightful to him "not so much because of its magnificent works and exquisite arts of antiquity as because of the records of its greatest men, where each of them lived, sat, and disputed,"[48] adding that he was then eagerly contemplating their tombs. I confess that this is strong incentive for encouraging one's natural talents, for rivalry acts as a great spur and, comparing oneself to one's predecessors and successors helps a man to become magnanimous.

We have read that a certain very great and slightly less extraordinary man said this: "He is sure that every very great man compares himself in his mind not only to those living at his own time, but also to outstanding men of every age."[49] Another spectacle, horrible but very effective for our salvation, is the opening of tombs, especially of those which are recent, and even more if they are of famous men, where one can see the effluence of worms, scattered entrails, bones removed from their resting places, noses eaten away, teeth knocked out, the cavities of eyes glazed over with slime, and hair matted with filth. O good Jesus! How much worse is that which we do not see! For who knows whether the soul is like the body and into what sort of abode it has been received if it has not found mercy?

The emperor Hadrian,[50] who was very interested in literature, expressed in a few words what scared him most about the journey of a departing soul. I am pleased to add these words so that they may display both the opinion and the compassion of such a great ruler, who continued to dictate until his last breath while others wept. Without doubt he spoke his mind because there was no reason to pretend. Addressing his own soul at his death, he said this: "Little soul, charming and wandering, guest and companion of my body, you now depart to places which are pale, stiff, and bare, nor will you tell jokes as you used to!"[51] I ask you: did he reveal too little of what he clearly felt and feared?

If the world, while it lasts, is like this for our leaders, and if such is their death, what should we think is the fate of others, for whom even life itself is a matter of daily toil? But humanity hears these things unwillingly, for by nature our minds avoid as much as possible any unpleasant and grievous thought. We imagine for ourselves delightful things, not torturous ones. Therefore, when we have grown old in the midst of hardships, we still do not cease betting on the happiness of the life which we have left behind; so great is the insistence of our desires that we prefer to wait for that which we know cannot happen, rather than pay attention courageously and wisely to that which we cannot bear.

In this matter countless people are deceived. Perhaps more truthfully, people knowingly and willingly fall into that agreeable error because we are eager to deceive ourselves. We are not diverted unless we are snatched, weeping, from opinions which are pleasing, but false. There are many false beliefs, but the greatest of them all was mentioned by Cicero in his *Tusculan Disputations,* that "each man hopes for Metellus' luck for himself."[52]

There is one greater and more dangerous madness: neither our nature nor so many constant examples persuade us to think about death. I do not believe that we have totally forgotten our mortality and weakness, but we prefer to avert our eyes so that we may not see it coming, as if it were safer not to see the enemy approaching. Therefore, we wait with eyes shut until he strikes. Surely everyone knows this weakness unless they pretend not to. Death, however, presses upon us, but when it is on our doorsteps, we flatter ourselves about its delay because the brevity of life makes death a neighbor, not just for an old man, but for a one-year-old as well. Its uncertainty makes it hang forever over our heads.

Nevertheless, I have testified with a loud voice that those who are not now willing to think of death will soon think about it, but, I greatly fear, will do so uselessly. I now end this chapter, for by my calculations we have come to the second part of today's discussion.

NOTES

1. Eccles. 1:2.
2. Eccles. 1:14.
3. Eccles. 2:1.
4. Eccles. 2:10.
5. Eccles. 2:11.
6. Eccles. 2:17-20.
7. Ecclus. 14:4.
8. It was Roman custom to pour out a small sip of wine as an offering to the gods before drinking it.
9. Horace, *Odes* 2.14.25-28.
10. Juvenal, *Satires* 14.137.
11. Ps. 38:6-7.
12. Ps. 48:11-12.
13. Ibid.
14. Ps. 48:13.
15. Ps. 48:15.
16. Gal. 6:14.
17. Claudian, *On the Fourth Consulate of Honorius* 299-300.
18. Ps. 68:2.
19. Ps. 57:8-9.
20. Ps. 121:2.
21. These are all rivers of the Graeco-Roman infernal regions.
22. In classical mythology Tantalus is punished in hell for the murder of his son by never being able to satisfy his hunger and thirst. For willing his soul to re-enter his own body and continue to live, Sisyphus has to push a rock up a hill, only to have it roll back down when he has almost completed his task. Ixion, who tried to rape Juno, the queen of the gods, was bound to a fiery, eternally-revolving wheel. The "crag of the Lapiths" may refer to the stone seat of forgetfulness on which the Lapith king Pirithous was forced to sit forever.
23. Ps. 11:9.
24. Ps. 82:14-15.
25. Ps. 34:6.
26. Cf. Seneca, *Epistles* 12.7.
27. Seneca, *Epistles* 58.2.
28. The River Sorgue, whose source is near Petrarch's home in Fontaine de Vaucluse.

29. Prosper of Aquitaine, "Poem of a Husband to His Wife" 35-36. Prosper (390–460) was believed to have been the author of a famous school book that bore his name. See also PL 51.612.

30. Prosper of Aquitaine, "Poem of a Husband to His Wife" 39-40.

31. Heraclitus of Ephesus (fl. 500 B.C.E.) believed that the basic stuff of the universe was fire and in constant motion.

32. Seneca, *Epistles* 58.23.

33. Dardanus was the founder of Troy, past which the River Xanthus flows. Romulus founded Rome, which lies along the River Tiber.

34. Seneca, *Epistles* 58.23.

35. Job 14:7, 9.

36. Job 14:10.

37. Job 14:11-12.

38. Job 14:12.

39. Job 6:15.

40. Petrarch, *On Human Affairs*.

41. The popes mentioned are Boniface VIII (1294–1303), John XXII (1316–1334), Clement V (1305–1314), and Clement VI (1342–52).

42. The German emperor referred to as Henry of Luxembourg (c.1276–1313) or Henry VII.

43. Petrarch refers to the following members of the French Capetian family: Philippe IV (r. 1285–1314), Louis X (r. 1314–1316), Philippe V (r. 1316–1322), Charles IV (r. 1322–1328), and to the members of the Valois family Philippe VI (r. 1328–1350) and John II (1350–1364).

44. The Spanish king is Alfonso XI (r. 1312–1350).

45. Robert of Anjou (c.1278–1343), the Wise, king of Naples and count of Provence, was much admired by Petrarch. On his death his granddaughter Joanna I seemed incapable of maintaining order in the kingdom.

46. Vergil, *Aeneid* 6.848.

47. Ps. 143:12.

48. Cicero, *On the Laws* 2.2.

49. Livy, on Scipio, *From the Founding of the City* 28.43.6.

50. Hadrian was the Roman emperor 117–138 C.E.

51. *The Augustan History,* The Life of Hadrian 25.

52. Cicero, *Tusculan Disputations* 1.36. The triumphs and political successes of the Metelli through the last three centuries of the Roman Republic are too numerous to determine which member of that clan Cicero means.

2

The seductions of the flesh still remain. I admit that these are difficult to overcome; nevertheless, it is possible, but only by divine assistance, for it is written in the book of Wisdom: "I have known that there is no other way for me to control my passions than for God to give me that ability."[1] In the light of such an authoritative witness, you know from Whom to seek such a wonderful gift. This knowledge is itself no insignificant gift of divine grace. This passage follows: "This itself was part of wisdom, to know Whose gift this was."[2] Therefore, my brothers, your self-reliance is in vain. You cannot stand up by yourselves. Your own strength cannot manage this task. The foul and heavy weight of the flesh presses and suffocates your poor weak soul by its own mass. This is your constant and insuperable affliction. You have, indeed, left the devil and the world, and you have closed yourselves off from both of them by the locked doors of your monastic retreat, but you cannot shut out the flesh.

Although St. Bernard used to encourage new initiates to leave their bodies behind them and enter as spirits, one should understand that the passions of this holy man and the "sharp goads" in his speech were intended to encourage a spiritual resolve and not a physical act. This encouragement is similar to the description of the agile soul's ascent to heaven in the sixth book of Cicero's *On the State:* "He will do this more easily if, still closed up in his body, he will venture to go outside it, and contemplating higher matters, he will detach himself from his body as much as possible."[3] Thus we must be joined to our bodies and inhabit them like pilgrims. Finally, consider Plato's universal idea in his *Phaedro:* "Philosophy is nothing other than the meditation of dying."[4] Here he means two deaths: one of our nature, the other of our virility. The first of these they say must neither be summoned nor feared, but awaited with calm. The second "death" should be sought with all eagerness, for it is this type of dying which your brothers have especially enjoyed, forgetting all desires and lusts, living in such a way in their body as if they had already escaped the prison of their limbs. So that we may persevere, we should often recall the teachings of philosophers and the encouraging words of St. Bernard.

Only by the power of nature, that is by death, can we truly leave behind our own flesh. We cannot do this while we are alive. Wherever we flee, it will follow us. Wherever we hide, it will find us. Humanity has neither rest nor complete freedom from worry until death because the same deceptions which adolescence or youth once renounced come back in old age with this enticing, complaining whine: "Where do you leave us if no return is possible? Where do you hope to find us again? Where there is no sleep, no food, no marriage? Why don't you enjoy yourselves while you can? Do not lose that time which you have been granted: it is very brief and slips by very quickly."

Anyone who observes that St. Augustine himself wavered, as he tells us in his *Confessions*, will be less surprised at the enticements of the flesh. Recall, too, St. Jerome, when he sat alone in his hermitage, drenched in bitter tears, exhausted by hair cloth, sleeplessness, hunger, and fasting, disgusting in his black squalor, in complete isolation from his fellow men, accompanied only by fearsome snakes and wild beasts. Despite the harshest conditions he still could not keep his pale and extremely emaciated body and his lustful mind from seething with empty carnal desires. He made that voluntary prison to keep his wandering mind from envisioning the dances of young girls, as he himself said, and other Roman delights, and to avoid the punishment of the eternal prison.[5] I name just those two men, whose genius, life, and faith cannot be ignored. Indeed, I could include the names of countless others.

So what must you fear to leave behind? Look at the first half of the speech of the dying Hadrian. My dearest brothers, I beg you to pay close attention to what he says: "Little soul, charming and wandering, guest and companion of my body." Alas! How many are those miserable and shameful enticements! What a wicked resting place! How evil is the connection between the body and the soul of the sinner! If only they all had to be enumerated, but that is not the case. Almost all of them are known to everyone. Between the body and the soul of a just man, however, there are no such enticements and no such love. Can anyone truly love such a formidable enemy? Certainly a wise man knows what sort of danger threatens him and realizes that this quote of Ovid is true: "A guest is not safe from his host."[6] What else was the Apostle Paul thinking when he wrote to the Romans, "I rejoice in the law of God regarding the inner man, but I see another law warring in my limbs with the law of my mind and bringing me into captivity of the law of sin, which is in my limbs."[7] This is surely that conflict of the body and soul about which he wrote to the Galatians: "The flesh has desires contrary to the spirit, and so does the spirit contrary to the flesh, for they are mutually opposed to each other."[8] Indeed, who would not fear that which he sees St. Paul fearing? Or who in such a difficult position would hope for help from anywhere else, except according to the advice of that Apostle: "The man who walks in the Spirit will not fulfill the desires of the flesh."[9] Because this cannot happen without the grace of God, as I have said, let him weep and fear with the same Apostle and say, "I am an unhappy person. Who will free me from the body of this death?"[10] Furthermore, when regaining his hope which comes only from the mercy of God, let him reply to himself: "The grace of God through Jesus Christ our Lord."[11]

Let us call out to the One Who alone is powerful enough to come to our rescue in this internal and personal battle. We must beg Him as suppliants to free us from the body of this death, from which we are freed, not by our own merit, but by the grace of God alone, to Whom nothing is difficult, not to mention impossible. Therefore, when we thirst as St. Paul did, let us hasten, as he did, to that fountain of mercy[12] lest we perish in our parched state. Let us even pray with that author of the book of Wisdom, who the Hebrews thought was Philo,[13] from whom we have learned that continence is the gift of God. Let us pray to the Bestower of such a great gift as this that He may send us from heaven "that wisdom which is the attendant in His own temple,"[14] not only for other matters, but also for the victory in this two-pronged war, so that "He may be with us and may work with us, and we may know what is acceptable to Him, for He knows and understands all those things, and He will lead us soberly in all our tasks and will guard us in His power."[15]

Our power is nothing. It is the power of weak men and limited time. Their "timid thoughts and uncertain foresight" and their "corruptible bodies burden our souls, their earth-bound life weighs down the mind which is thinking many things."[16]

If the wisdom of God abandons anyone who seems perfect, that man is considered as nothing. In the present struggle of our flesh, we will gain strength through this wisdom, my brothers, and we will be victorious and cleansed of all sin. Having been set straight, we will be saved. As the same wise man says, it is through this wisdom that "whoever has pleased God from the beginning has been made whole."[17] This is the way you must walk to conquer the flesh which you have been unable to leave behind. As St. Paul said to the Corinthians, "When you walk in the flesh, do not take up arms according to the flesh."[18] This is as difficult as it is worthy of a great reward, but in this matter, just as in all the other wars of mortals, if earthly frailty feels the presence of the aid of heaven somewhat more, the victory and triumph come from God in both instances, but especially in this one.

Indeed, brothers, we know Babylon's many rivers which we must cross with great danger. Seeking the right hand of our Lord in crossing them, let us cry out with a Christian voice to the One Who is truly unconquered. We shall cry out as [the soul of] Vergil's shipwrecked Palinurus [in the underworld] did to his master, who had been truly conquered and exiled [from Troy]: "Rescue me from these evils.... Give your right hand to this miserable man and lift me with you through the waves so that I may at least lie in death in a calm resting place."[19] Or, if you prefer a religious quotation, let us cite that line from David: "Save me, O Lord, since the waters have entered all the way to my soul," and then: by His aid let us be plucked up "as from the slime of the deep and the depths of the sea."[20] No river, however, is longer or swifter than this one, which my pen now paddles.

More than my own experience, which instructs me in all things, I can attribute this depth of understanding to the authority of learned men as well. Cicero said, "The pleasure of the body flows and soon vanishes, leaving behind a motive for repentance more often than a motive for remembrance."[21] Severinus Boethius said, "Every desire has this: it drives the impetuous with its whips, it flees away like flying bees, and it stings our hearts with a deep bite."[22]

If one seeks stability, consider the nature of the river of Babylon: it flows off and flees. Both these actions are appropriate, for the word "river" takes its name from "flow."[23] Neither one says anything new: we have heard that desire is "flowing" and "fleeting," but we knew this long ago. That was already enough, even if there were nothing worse, but in the end when I hear the reason for repentance and see the vexation of the spirit and the long bitterness which follows brief pleasure, I ask what could be less befitting to a wise man than uselessly wanting something of which he will immediately repent? Remarkably, St. Paul said the same thing in his letter to the Romans: "Just as you have offered your limbs to serve filth and one wrong after another, so now offer your limbs to serve righteousness and holiness, for when you were slaves of sin, you were free from goodness."[24] Then he added to those words something most persuasive: "What enjoyment did you have then in those things over which you now blush? The end of those things is death, but now having become free from sin, having been made slaves of God, you have your enjoyment in holiness and, moreover, an end in eternal life. The wages of sin are death, but the grace of God is eternal life in our Lord Jesus Christ."[25]

Who would hesitate, my friends, among these choices? Would one prefer to be disgraced or holy? Death or eternal life? If the choice is clear, one must not waver as to whether to obey the flesh or the spirit. Corruption and death come from the former, while holiness and eternal life grow from the latter.

It is fitting to add one related saying of a very wise Gentile. I make no changes in any part, but cite the exact words of the oration delivered by Marcus Cato to his soldiers at Numantia[26]: "Think in your minds if you have done anything correctly through your effort: that effort will quickly depart from you, but its benefit will not leave you while you live; if you have acted basely at any time through desire, the desire will quickly go away, but that which you have done basely will always remain with you."[27] "Always" is a better word than "while you live,"[28] especially for us, who have been persuaded that the works of the living follow the dead, that neither pains nor rewards cease with death. Many writings, which the brevity of this tome does not encompass, indicate that pagans too were convinced of this, although not so strongly. Maybe something more flowery can be said than this exhortation of Cato which I have cited, but nothing, I judge, could be truer or more thought-provoking.

So, my brothers, let us stop here, wholly mindful of the teachings of the Apostles and the advice of philosophers. Let each man look inside himself. If he has done anything in his life virtuously, how much glory and delight did he receive? If he has done anything lustfully and basely, how much shame, repentance, and grief have resulted? Out of the memory of those things which have passed, let him choose what he ought to do or what he ought to avoid. Let him compare the immensity of his baseness with its negligible enjoyment, or more realistically with no enjoyment at all. Let him also consider the ruin of his reputation and the loss of his body and soul. Let him keenly direct his thoughts to the devil, who deceives mortal eyes with soothing pretense and sells at so great a price a person's flesh to those who trade in the world. Let him look deeply into the heart of things so that he may learn to condemn appearances. Let him not pay service to lust, but to his salvation. In all matters, let him consider the passing of the present, being mindful of the beginning and looking forward to the end. Let him remember his shame, knowing that he sees himself more clearly in the shadows, however dark, than in the light. Let him direct all his thoughts to the pursuit of virtue, rejecting all those enticing attractions with strength and sternness.

Let a young man consider chastity a most becoming prize. Let an elderly man consider lust the foulest part of old age. Let the handsome man know that beauty wars against chastity. Let the deformed man know that the mind itself is deformed by sin. Let the former man beware deformity; let the latter man desire beauty in the man who dwells within. Let a boy know that he has now begun; let an older man know that he has not yet finished. Let the former undertake the care of his long life; let the latter not put aside the concerns which he has taken up. Let the rich man seek praise for continence; let the poor man avoid the infamy of lust. Let a monk know that reason for shame resides not only under his hair-shirt, but also in his mind. Let soft thoughts be banished from your stern threshold; let delicate desires be banished from your hard beds.

Contemplate the words of St. Paul, who was the sharpest spur for St. Augustine to change his life, as is well known from his own writing[29]: "Not in eating and drinking, in beds and scandals, in strife and pretense, but dress yourselves in our Lord Jesus Christ and the sacrifice of His flesh lest you act upon your desires."[30] If this is said to everyone, however, what is said especially to you, who of all those in Christ's army profess these ideals with the strictest oath? If anything more enticing creeps in with stealth, how easily, I hope, it will disappear, once confronted with the character of your dwelling and your firm resolve. Indeed, if a particular location incites luxurious living, a situation which we read that Cicero condemned in Verres,[31] why would it not call for purity of body? Would the same place not encourage good things any less than evil ones?

How different is the rigor of your hermitage from the softness of the flesh? Carnal desire is a very pleasurable thing. It is nourished by sleep, rest, and food. It is enticed by soft clothing and choice apparel, by secret whispers, by joy, by jokes and songs. It hates and flees difficulties. It has, therefore, neither a resting place in your rugged and harsh quarters nor any commerce with your sleepless, laborious, fasting, and vigorous brotherhood, which always praises God with sad sighing and ponderous tones.

We know, however, that Christ, a just man, suffered for us, who are unjust. He did this so that He might restore to God those of us who, although mortified in the flesh, are alive in spirit. So let us hope and pray that the death of our Lord in this world may free us from eternal death, and that death may be the death of this flesh and the destruction of our sins so that His Resurrection may be the life of our souls and eventually even of our bodies. Let Him take pity on the afflicted, bring aid to the needy, and offer His hand to the weary. We suffer a heavy burden while we are alive (or rather while we are said to be alive), while we are here, while the comeliness of our renewed soul is often suddenly and secretly splattered with old stains, and while the disgraces of youth, enveloped by the mantle of long habit, ingrain themselves again in us and pursue us in our tired and exhausted old age. Consequently, if our divine Guard did not expose our plots by sounding the alarm, we would relapse into those old sins which we had previously cast off behind our backs. Therefore, prostrating ourselves with tears, let us say, "Take away the disgrace which I dread."[32] Together let us cry out, "Unveil my eyes, and I will contemplate the wonders of Your law."[33]

We have discovered, however, that no curtain veils the eyes of the soul from contemplating divinity as much as the fog raised by a cloud of desires. This truth was first seen by Socrates, the parent of philosophy, that discipline which pertains especially to life and morals, and then by his student Plato, the most excellent philosopher before all others, who is the one most suited to our faith. Vergil later clothed this truth in poetic disguise. St. Augustine and many other Christian scholars acknowledge the deceit of desire with more words than the matter really requires.

Is there anyone living, angels aside, who has undergone the assaults and treacheries of the flesh, who is not absolutely certain of these two things? First, who does not know that God, Who is seen only by the purest eyes, is not seen when lust commands; and second, that lustful men do not "consider the wonders which come from His law."[34] Lust commands that there be no place for rational thought nor, consequently, for humanity, which cannot exist nor be understood without rational thought. Human nature itself is undone when the mind turns savage and arrives at such misery that it turns God's most illustrious gift of rational thought into dark and base indulgence in desires. Such men become "like the horse and mule, in whom there is no understanding."[35] Rational thought has been given to humanity from heaven. It is a gift by which He commands all living creatures.

Among no other living creatures is passion so varied, as I have said. Although this matter is so well known, as every person is a witness for himself, nevertheless it is pleasing to introduce the testimony of a very famous man. It may be widely known and thus may seem superfluous to many, but to you, who live in your hermitage and are dedicated solely to the pursuit of sacred writings, perhaps it will be welcome, by its novelty and certainly by its authority, its truth, and its very variety. By this study, just as in writing prose I sometimes season my pen for a secular audience with religious citations, so I am delighted by secular references (which were my first and for some time my only reading) when my audience consists of clerics and monks. These works, where they agree with our works, add a suitable, if fleeting, support.

Consider Archytas of Tarentum.[36] He was by far the first and greatest of the Italian philosophers after Pythagoras, so great that Plato (himself the chief Greek philosopher) sailed to Italy to visit him. Archytas confirms by the authority of his own testimony those very serious matters which we have discussed. Lest I lose anything said by Cicero, I quote directly: "He said that no more deadly plague has been given to mortals by nature than the pleasure of the body, and that in order to gain control of the body, avid desires are incited recklessly and uncontrollably. From such desires arise those who betray their country, overthrow their states, and deal clandestinely with the enemy. In short, there is no crime nor wickedness that the lust of pleasure does not impel us to undertake. Rape, adultery, and all such offenses are stirred up by no other enticements than those of pleasure. Because either nature or some god has given humanity nothing better than his mind, nothing is so inimical to this divine favor and gift than pleasure. There is no place for temperance when lust has the upper hand, nor can virtue reside at all in the realm of pleasure. To make this clearer, he ordered one to think about a person aroused by as much pleasure of the body as can possibly be imagined. He thought nobody would have any doubt that while that person was enjoying himself for so long, he could do nothing with his mind nor accomplish anything with reason and reflection. Therefore nothing is so detestable and so deadly as pleasure if indeed, when it is greater or of longer duration, it can blot out all the light of the soul."[37]

This is the opinion of Archytas which I explained to you in the words of Cicero, and if the worth of such witnesses adds any weight, Cicero likewise tells us that Archytas spoke these words with the father of that Pontius, who defeated the Roman army (without a wound, contrary to custom!) at the battle of the Caudine Forks,[38] that is Gaius Pontius, the commander of the Samnites, a man who not even his enemies have denied was the wisest of that age. He also spoke with the philosopher Plato, who I know was always a man of the most zealous disposition for learning, as St. Augustine says,[39] both a wandering student of the most famous teacher of Athens and a pursuer of universal knowledge, as St. Jerome says,[40] or its collector and in turn its disperser, as Valerius says.[41] What keeps me from believing that he learned from Archytas the Platonic opinion about pleasure which I have put forth above? It is often the custom of eager and persistent geniuses to make an opinion their own by treating and meditating on it, especially since Plato became such a friend to Archytas that I believe he dedicated books to Archytas out of admiration for his genius.

Whosoever's opinion it was, mindful of the Academy,[42] I do not hesitate to assert that it was one of a number of those ideas most true among so many dubious ones. Rightly, therefore, every day we pray: "Unveil my eyes."[43] In so doing, we ask God to remove the veil which keeps us from the sight and contemplation of the heavens and holds us to this earth. "Stay awake, therefore, and pray,"[44] most beloved brothers, "singing praises, call upon the Lord, and you will be saved from your enemies."[45] Make the best of your leisure, and you will find knowledge. Make time, and you will see that to which you aspire, and strive to remove whatever stands in your way.

Whether we consider our soul or our body, our reputation or our inheritance (which I count among the least important), or our time on earth, which is said to be and is indeed irretrievable, the obstacles which lust puts forth are certainly numerous and huge. There is little or no enjoyment in the flaw of the flesh. "What good is there in my blood if I descend into corruption?"[46] Most appropriately the Psalmist says, "I descend," for there is nowhere any cliff so steep, any abyss so precipitous, any base of so lofty a mountain, from which there can be so great and so frightening a descent as that from the summit of innocence into the abyss of sin, not even if someone should fall headfirst into the source of the River Sorgue far below from the top of this cliff which looms over me as I write these words. If my power of estimating is functioning, nothing is higher than this cliff, for I have not seen anything steeper.[47]

❧　❧　❧

NOTES

1. Wisd. 8:21.
2. Ibid.
3. Cicero, *On the State* 6.29.
4. Plato, *Phaedro* 67d.
5. Jerome, *Epistles* 22.7.
6. Ovid, *Metamorphoses* 1.144.
7. Rom. 7:22-23.
8. Gal. 5:17.
9. Gal. 5:16.
10. Rom. 7:24.
11. Rom. 7:25.
12. Cf. Heb. 4:16.
13. Philo of Alexandria (c.20 B.C.E.–c.42 C.E.) was a major Jewish theologian and biblical exegete. See also Jerome, *Preface to the Books of Solomon,* PL 28.1308.
14. Wisd. 9:4.
15. Wisd. 9:10-11.
16. Wisd. 9:14-15.
17. Wisd. 9:19.
18. 2 Cor. 10:3.
19. Vergil, *Aeneid* 6.365, 370.
20. Ps. 68:2-3.
21. Cicero, *On the Ends of Good and Evil* 2.106.
22. Boethius, *Consolation of Philosophy* 3.7.
23. The Latin word for "river," *flumen,* is derived from the verb "to flow," *fluo, fluere.*
24. Rom. 6:19-20.
25. Rom. 6:21-23.
26. The Romans besieged Numantia in 133 B.C.E., in the last battle in their conquest of Spain.
27. Aulus Gellius, *Attic Nights* 16.1.4.
28. Cf. Apoc. 14.11.
29. Augustine, *Confessions* 8.12.
30. Rom. 13:13-14.

31. Cicero prosecuted Verres, the former Roman governor of Sicily, for greedily plundering that province.

32. Ps. 118:39.

33. Ps. 118:18.

34. Ibid.

35. Ps. 31:9.

36. Archytas of Tarentum (first half of 4th century B.C.E.) was a mathematician and philosopher.

37. Cicero, *On Old Age* 39-41.

38. 321 B.C.E. in the Second Samnite War between the Romans and the Samnites, who lived in the mountainous region south of the Roman district of Latium.

39. Augustine, *City of God* 8.4.

40. Jerome, *Epistles* 53.1.

41. Valerius Maximus 8.7, ext. 3.

42. The Academy refers generally to the philosophic successors of Plato, but specifically to the moderate skeptical tradition associated with the Academy in its later stages.

43. Ps. 118:18.

44. Matt. 26:41.

45. Ps. 17:4.

46. Ps. 29:10.

47. A visitor to Petrarch's Museum at Fontaine de Vaucluse immediately appreciates the precipitous nature of the cliffs rising above Petrarch's head at the source of the River Sorgue.

3

E ven though I would say that this matter is too certain and obvious to have to be proven or shown, nevertheless, to demonstrate further that no usefulness or enjoyment follows such a descent, or more truly, such ruin, let me say what this concern recalls to my mind.

Now listen to the words of another pagan, Scipio Africanus. He is less well remembered in literature than the other two Scipios, but he was greater in deeds as well as handsome, and young, qualities hostile to true morality. He was speaking to Masinissa, a great friend of his and of the Roman people.[1] Masinissa had been enticed by the beauty and allure of the woman [Sophonisba] whom he married, although she was the wife of his enemy [Syphax], a king who was held captive. Thus their marriage was neither legal nor rightful. Having publicly praised Masinissa for deeds which he had energetically and bravely accomplished in battle, Scipio led him into a secluded place, where, having chastised the young king's wantonness, whether more discretely or effectively I know not, he told him: "Get control of yourself; do not spoil your many good deeds with one vice, and do not corrupt the gratitude which we feel for your many services with guilty actions graver than their cause."[2]

O what an outstanding statement! It is worthy more of an old man than a young military leader. One might think it worthy of a buskin-clad poet, a pallium-clad philosopher, or even an apostle! "With guilty actions graver," he says, "than their cause." As for all those who are inclined to sin, especially to lust, how I wish that they could consider and examine the merits of this saying so that when their flesh is aroused, their mind may be reined in by this thought to restrain their actions!

I certainly am not saying that a body which has been unrestrained since its youth is easily reined in after it has grown up in pleasure and freedom. It has been written that "whoever delicately nourishes his slave from boyhood will later feel his obstinacy."[3] The flesh, or rather this little donkey of ours, is our slave, nourished in the soft, happy pasture of desire, lying between those rivers about which we have said many things. Accustomed to the wide, flat paths of this world, why has the lazy creature not gone forth to climb Mount Zion, up to whose peak there leads a steep, narrow, and craggy pathway? What sort of cure is there, except that the older we are, the more painfully, forcefully, and zealously we have to devote ourselves to this so that, by unlearning its familiar surroundings, we may get to know something different. The task is harsh and laborious, I confess, but good for us, for certainly if we wish to be saved, that little donkey which we now goad must be reined in and beaten so that it will not drag us down with it as it stubbornly indulges in its usual licentiousness.

We have seen, heard, and read about certain people who have accomplished this, especially those two outstanding men who scorned the temptations of this world, the monk Hilarion and St. Francis. Hilarion fought against the flames of desire with noble disdain like a man while he was scarcely a youth. St. Jerome tells us that he was so angry at himself that he beat his chest with his fists as if he could drive out such thoughts with the striking of his hands. "You little beast," he said, "I'll make you not be so stubborn. I'll not feed you with barley, but with straw, and I will afflict you with hunger and thirst, I will burden you with a heavy weight, I will track you through heat and cold so that you think about food rather than pleasure."[4] St. Francis is reputed to have said and done likewise, for he called his own body his donkey. He buried himself naked at night in a mass of snow and overcame the vile fires of desire with the glorious passion of his mind and the coldness of his flesh.

You should follow these examples, my brothers. We should hold to this course and assail our donkey with a bridle, deprive it of food, oppress and chafe it with heavy backpacks, and finally rebuke it and reduce it to obedience in every way.[5] If that heavenly man St. Paul accomplished this, what do we think we should do? Must we stand in arms and like a worldly army spend the winter under skin garments? Must we pray not just three times, but a thousand times, that our feisty attitude be taken away from us? If we are answered in our inner ear as was St. Paul, what else is there to do but "rejoice in our infirmities so that the virtue of Christ may come to dwell in us as well."[6] I hope you will be granted what was denied to Paul, that "the magnitude of his revelations not exalt" him.[7]

Accordingly then, my brothers, direct your thoughts to this ongoing and dangerous struggle which is being waged with our flesh, our domestic enemy. Work hard, stay on guard, listen for every noise, and fully armed, jump into the fight. There are no truces in this battle as there are in all other wars. Many things constantly imperil our salvation and the things that are most important to us. Our battle is with the most deceitful enemy. We are driven by force and by treachery in so many different directions because sometimes he appears to be a real enemy, and at others he pretends to be our friend. What is more changeable and enticing, but more insidious than desire? Those who have experienced it know it. What mature human being of sound body has not experienced it? As for the rest, the more determined the enemy, the more celebrated is the victory.

Cicero said, "The enticements of a very flattering mistress twist great parts of our mind from virtue."[8] Seneca said, "Above all, thrust away desires and consider them most hateful; they embrace us like bandits, whom the Egyptians call assassins, so that they can strangle us."[9] So it is.

All other evils strike us as if they were coming head-on. Determined to make us unhappy, luxury surrounds us, so we must resist it as it comes. We must meet these evils as soon as they appear, and we must keep that saying in our thoughts: "Blessed shall he be who will take his own little ones and strike them against a rock."[10] Of course, we should understand these "little ones" as new, little, and newly-born thoughts, which we are warned to strike against a rock before they can grow up, overcome us, and armed with experience, fling us down from our citadel of rational thought: "The rock, however, was Christ."[11]

Who, I beseech you, will ever be of such indomitable or inflamed lust that he would not grow cold at the memory of Christ's wounds and at the thought that His blood was poured out for this purpose above all, that the ingrained filth of our wounds might thereby be washed away? His blood is even better for extinguishing or calming human passions, provided it flows into a devout soul who beseeches Him from a lofty cloud of fervid contemplation. No rain or dew is so invigorating for dry grass as this. Nevertheless, I ask: who is so inhumane and ungrateful, reflecting upon the horrible death of his father, master, or friend, a death which we accept hoping for salvation, that he would not forget his own desires and be turned from pointless and base happiness to beautiful tears? And yet all these things are possible in Christ.

What else did that vision of Isaiah mean, which begins, "Hear, O Heaven, and give an ear, O earth, for the Lord has spoken: 'I have nourished and exalted your sons. They have scorned me.'"[12] Lo, I say, we have briefly heard our Father and our Lord: surely He is the same One Who makes Himself our Friend. "You are My friends," He says, "I will no longer call you My slaves."[13] He calls us His friends; let us acknowledge Him as our Lord.

Certain masters have the custom of treating their slaves as part of their family, conversing with them pleasantly, tolerating much, forgiving much, divulging much, and hiding much. Such masters should not be feared any less, but loved more. I am aware that some foolish slaves have contempt for a master's familiarity, but when such a master is grievously wounded, they do become angry and usually avenge an insult more severely than those who get angry slowly. Who could be gentler than Christ, who said, "Learn from Me that I am gentle and humble in My heart"?[14] How much more directly has our heavenly Father said this to us than Aeneas said to his son: "My boy, learn virtue from me."[15] What virtue do you mean, O son of Anchises? Was it the betrayal of your country, although you may be absolved of this by Vergil's eloquence, a betrayal which certain poets and historians totally ignored, not even mentioning the house of Priam in their opinions? Did you not make sacrifices to demons with the slaughter and blood of your friends? Christ, however, the true Father and Lord and Teacher and our God, by His own law teaches that we should learn from Him, not those virtues which we cannot imitate, but those befitting human nature, for He teaches us to be gentle and humble of heart. He certainly would have sent us to learn this elsewhere if He had found any clearer example of gentleness.

Can it be that His unutterable and infinite grace is not well enough known to all who hope in Him? Daily He awaits us, calls us, arouses us, warns us, encourages us, and summons us, through messengers, through Scripture, and through Himself. He beckons, "Come to me, you who labor and are burdened."[16] He offers us rest from labors, and promises consolation from grief, pardon for sins, hope for better times, and, in the end, everlasting life. "Let the ungodly man abandon his way, and let the unjust man abandon his thoughts and return to the Lord, and He will have mercy on him, and to God, since He is great in His forgiveness."[17] And again: "In the same way a father forgives his sons, so the Lord has had compassion for those who fear Him."[18] What could be more soothing than this statement?

Beware, O sinner, lest He become angry! He says: "If, however, they shall have abandoned My laws and will not walk in My judgment, if they profane My ordinances and do not keep My commandments, I will punish their iniquities with My rod and their sins with My blows. But I will not remove My mercy from them."[19] Here too, what could be more calming than this strictness? Let Him threaten with His rod and His blows, not His sword nor His axe: this is the threat of a father, not of the courts. He chastises us and by that chastising He does not destroy us, but He has mercy on us and corrects us because He Himself knows our creation and remembers that we are but dust. Still gentle and patient, "merciful and compassionate is our Lord, long-suffering and compassionate."[20]

Beware not to push Him too much nor to expect too much because elsewhere it is written: "If I shall sharpen My sword like lightning, if My hand shall take hold of judgment, I will execute vengeance on my enemies, and I will punish those who hate Me."[21] Behold! Now you have nothing gentle or paternal, but quite legal and strict, for He does not now address sons, friends, or even slaves, but His enemies. Now there is no mention of rods and blows. But what? "I will imbue My arrows with blood, and My sword will devour flesh from the gore of those whom I have killed and from My bare-headed, captive enemies."[22]

This is not the chastising of a father, I tell you, but hostile vengeance: slaughter and captivity, sword and arrows. There is also nothing more threatening than what He says in the same Psalm: "A fire has been lit by My anger and will burn all the way to the depths of hell."[23] Behold how suddenly He changes significantly His plans for the sons of humanity. Suddenly He grows angry. We have to seize the chance for forgiveness lest His sudden anger seize us. "When His anger burns briefly, all those who trust in Him will be blessed."[24] Surely real trust does not arise except from truth. Let us cultivate the truth to gain that trust which in the midst of unexpected dangers renders us fearless and blessed.

What other sort of remedy is there, my brothers, or what are the tools of victory in which we can put our trust in this war? Where can we place our hope? Can we trust in a vast supply of wealth? In kingdoms and power that must end? Or in the power of our limbs and the strength of our bodies? Or in horses, chariots, and war machinery? Banish all these from our soul! They are not the paths to salvation. Let it not be us about whom just men laugh and say: "Look, there is someone who did not claim God as his helper, but put his hope in the mass of his riches and grew strong in his vanity."[25] We know that "a king is not saved by great virtue, nor will a giant be saved by the immensity of his strength."[26] We know that "a war-horse is a vain hope for salvation."[27] We know that "he will not delight in the strength of a horse nor will he find satisfaction in a man's legs."[28] But what is our King's purpose, by which our weakness can be redeemed? Surely we also know that: "The Lord finds His pleasure in those who fear Him and in those who place their hopes in His mercy."[29] This is the most direct path to salvation, and we must follow it:

"not in our bow shall we put our hopes, nor is it our sword that will save us,"[30] but "the right hand of God, His arm, and the light of His countenance."[31] Here we must pin our hopes, hither we must turn our minds, hence we must seek help. "Some call on their chariots, some their horses, but we will invoke the name of God,"[32] knowing that "fruitless is salvation by human means; in God we will fight valiantly, and He Himself will annihilate our enemies."[33] This, not anything else, is our salvation. This is our strength. This is our security. This is our only remedy against the wrath of the Lord: to make time, to fear, to hope, and to pray that in His fury He will not censure us, nor in His wrath punish us,"[34] but let Him keep that wrath far from us "and remove His blows."[35] Meanwhile we have to live in such a way that we earn His attention and His mercy.[36] Without doubt His mercy is to be loved, and His justice feared. Let us appease His justice with good deeds and beg for His mercy with godly prayers.[37]

However, so that I may return to my subject, if anyone of a devout mind remembers that this Lord, be He gentle or fearsome, suffered such things for him, all the spurs of lust will be broken, and although deeply fixed in the flesh, they will spring out after it is conquered. No thought is more useful than the thought of one's own death, nor has it been said without purpose: "Be mindful of your end, and you will not sin for eternity."[38] It will help us to have a mind constantly well-trained and armed with these remedies. Always on our guard, we will fight against the fires of the flesh, for there is no scourge more dangerous, none more frequent, none more common. It holds sway over every race of humanity. It arouses every walk of life, bothers both sexes, and penetrates into every age. Where other scourges plague individuals, this one plagues everyone.

There is a story, by no means inelegant, that the devil brought forth seven daughters from an unspeakable intercourse with a sinning soul: Pride, Avarice, Gluttony, Anger, Jealousy, Sloth, and Luxury. When he had put them all in order for marriage, individual ones for different groups of people, whose names I will not mention lest my freely-flowing pen may by chance offend someone, only the youngest daughter Luxury remained unwed, and because she was more enticing than all her sisters, she was sought by everyone and limited by no specific bonds of marriage, but publicly prostituted. The result was that, while the other vices belong to individual races, as I have said, she alone belongs to them all. She is there at all times and in all places, wherever we turn, either as a living form, as an ornament dazzling to the eyes, as an enticing voice falling on our ears, or as some allurement always awaiting our senses. She not only provokes war openly in the middle of the day, but she dares to break into shadows and hiding places. Rather she recovers her boldness in hidden places and rages even more licentiously on a stormy night; finally, when dark plagues are lulled to sleep, she keeps watch and makes human repose restless. Portents in dreams and turbulent visions declare that this is true.

If great minds dispute the nature of these visions, I believe, nevertheless, that we have not yet quite reached the heart of the matter. Their appearances are so many; the shapes of them are so varied; our rest is beset so often for no reason, or certainly for unknown reasons. All kinds of things occur in our dreams which we have never considered nor would ever have considered. What these seven vices will not dare to do when we are awake, they do when we are asleep. Sometimes they stir up thoughts in us which we would oppose were we awake, and when we awaken, we weep. When the soul is overwhelmed in sleep and almost inebriated, they drag it with their tricks where it could never be dragged, even with open force, when it is awake and sober. St. Augustine himself, already advanced both in sanctity and age, lamented this mockery of sleep.[39]

Moderation in all things and, even more, a soberness of the soul offers much against those hidden and (as I have said before) subconscious attacks. Hunger, toil, and watchfulness, which provoke deep sleep that even wipes out dreams, have the same effect. Control of the mind, which enables us to dismiss base thoughts and meaningless matters, is the soul's best form of protection, for it helps us to redirect our attention to the good, true, and stable concept of the covenant about which Job said, "I have made a pact with my eyes that they would not even consider a maiden."[40] He did not say that they would not *see*, but that they would not *consider*. What good is it to have turned away one's eyes, or to have closed them, or even to have lost them, if our wandering mind sometimes stands in awe at sights of former lust and if free thought is given license to wander where our bodily sensations cannot? Indeed, if nothing at all except what the eye sees were to arouse passionate desires, night and darkness would have a good deal of innocence, whereas each of them burns with its own desires, and night with even greater ones.

Therefore we must control and restrain our minds. Our thought process must be brought in line with something like shackles, but because

Scripture teaches us "death enters through the windows,"[41] so those thoughts must be closed off, or guarded by an alert watchman. This is why a covenant must be made with our eyes for the salvation of our soul so that our eyes may not open up a path for dangerous sights, and so that the soul may stay on guard at the threshold and, even though the doors be open, prevent troops of fantasies from entering: in other words, to have subjected the flesh to the spirit and to have overcome oneself. No victory is more illustrious than this. We attain it with these special weapons, which I have mentioned previously: frugality of life, meditation on death, affliction of the body, humility of the soul, circumspection and watchfulness, retreat from women, roughness of clothing, memory of the suffering of Christ, anticipation of the Last Judgment, fear of hell, and hope of eternal life.

Countless examples of this idea suffice from the stories of the saints. There are truly as many subduers of the flesh as there are saints. I will not mention St. Paul, who even in his own case is a most believable witness. Others include St. Anthony, Hilarion, and Ambrose, who excelled in mastering themselves, as the biographies of those men testify, but nobody was more outstanding than St. Francis. This is the way, and these saints are our guides. Our goal is to have an obedient body and a free soul, nay, one which rules, for such a soul can be put in God's service.

As usually happens in warfare, so too in this battle of life, if in good faith a person has put an end to his former troubles, he will have sounded the end of battle. I think that he will be free from these storms either completely or for the most part, especially if daily fasting and silence, faithful evening prayer and undoubting hope of divine assistance are his lot. Obviously all these endeavors, which I have listed one at a time, will be more familiar to you than to any other men, for the rigor and solitude of your training imposes experiences which other men usually seek with great effort. I beseech you to have a sense of balance and be mindful of your purpose.

⁊   ⁊   ⁊

NOTES

1. Publius Cornelius Scipio (236–184/3 B.C.E.) led the Romans in Spain and Africa during the second half of the Second Punic War (218–201 B.C.E.). After his defeat of Hannibal at the battle of Zama (202 B.C.E.), Scipio was given the honorary title "Africanus." There were several other Cornelius Scipios of great military renown in the third and second centuries B.C.E. Masinissa was the king of Numidia, the kingdom immediately to the west of Carthage.

2. Livy, *From the Founding of the City* 30.14.11. Petrarch dedicated the fifth book of his *Africa* to retelling this story.

3. Prov. 29:21.

4. Jerome, *Life of Hilarion*, PL 23.32.

5. Cf. 1 Cor. 9:27.

6. 2 Cor. 12:9.

7. 2 Cor. 12:7.

8. Cicero, *On Duties* 2.37.

9. Seneca, *Epistles* 51.13.

10. Ps. 136:9.

11. 1 Cor. 10:4.

12. Isa. 1:2.

13. John 15:14-15.

14. Matt. 11.29.

15. Vergil, *Aeneid* 12.435.

16. Matt 11:28.

17. Isa. 55:7.

18. Ps. 102:13.

19. Ps. 88:31-34.

20. Ps. 102:8.

21. Deut. 32:41.

22. Deut. 32:42.

23. Deut. 32:22.

24. Ps. 2:13.

25. Ps. 51:9.

26. Ps. 32:16.

27. Ps. 32:17.

28. Ps. 146:10.
29. Ps. 146:11.
30. Ps. 43:7.
31. Ps. 43:4.
32. Ps. 19:8.
33. Ps. 107:13-14.
34. Ps. 6:2, 37:2.
35. Ps. 38:11.
36. Cf. Petrarch, *Remedies* 1.8.
37. Ibid. 2.58.
38. Ecclus. 7:40.
39. Augustine, *Confessions* 10.30.
40. Job 31:1.
41. Jer. 9:21.

4

We could say much about the brevity of life, the predictability of unpredictable death, the impurity of the flesh, the vileness of sin, the glory of virtue, and those eternal punishments and rewards which distract the mind from evil desires. On one hand, the mind is dumbfounded by its perils and scared by the moral impurity of useless delights, and on the other, it is intrigued by difficult challenges and compares the tasks of this life to tomorrow's rewards. Everyone knows this, however, and this little book is beginning to grow beyond its purpose. Therefore, so that the end may echo the beginning: "Take time and," what follows, "see."[1] What, really, will you see? He says "that I am God, so you will see the God of gods on Zion."[2]

Nevertheless, if we want to arrive at that vision beyond which there is absolutely nothing to which our minds or those of angels can aspire, I ask you: down which paths should we walk? Should we walk through greed and temporary profits? Through lust, luxury, and meaningless joy? Through pride, anger, and bloody battles? I would like to stop here for a while, for this matter is worth understanding, and a sober traveler ought to ask the correct path. Indeed, according to Gentile writers, many people (especially Romulus and Hercules) have gone to heaven down these paths, but I do not understand how they could spread their wings for such a great flight. The former was soaked in the blood of his brother, the other in the blood of many. Where are Castor and Pollux[3] and the Roman Caesars, who have been deified because of their deeds, the greatness of their empire, the glory of their wars, and especially because of the unbelievable credulity of their subjects? Has the Truth not drowned these same men in the depths of hell?

Did Cicero not confess this clearly enough? Indeed, he said, "We have exalted this city's founder Romulus to the immortal gods because of our affection for him and desire to glorify him,"[4] which is certainly nothing other than to have exalted him by a lie. He offers a weak case when he says "affection" and confesses the false deification when he says "to glorify him." It was not the merit of the man, but the favor of his citizens and their love, the parent of false judgment, which impelled them to confer a false kind of divinity on that blood-stained king, a divinity which was given to him, not by truth, but by a desire to glorify, which is the progenitor of untruth. Behold a lifeless god, taken up to heaven (as the

Roman senator Proculus Julius believed when he returned from the countryside), but in reality killed and cut to pieces by the senators and then thrown into the Goat's Marsh so that no trace of the murder would remain.[5] These are the "secrets of the deified Romulus,"[6] whom the affection of the common people unreasonably glorifies, whom tenuous fame deifies and elevates to heaven. This is the real meaning of that proclamation of Cicero which I just cited: "We have exalted him to heaven by affection and glorification."

In his zeal for truth in this matter, Cicero did not fear the animosity of the common people. Some may find this rather vague, but what he wrote in his work *On Duties* is very clear: "It was not such in the case of the king who founded this city," he says. "The notion of expediency controlled his mind: when it seemed more advantageous to him to rule alone rather than with another, he killed his own brother."[7] Romulus set aside any feeling of piety and humanity so that he could attain what he thought was utility, but it was not. He treated the wall as a matter of honor, which was neither an acceptable nor a sufficiently adequate explanation. So begging the pardon either of Quirinus[8] or of Romulus, I would say that a sin was committed. Mindful of his profession, Cicero almost forgets courteousness in his words: with the freedom of a philosopher, he argues like a foreigner that the people should fear the founder of their city, and he strips bare the life, not of a god, but of an impious and wicked man.

What do the historians say? What do the poets themselves say, to whose songs brave men owe whatever fame they have, not only about fictitious deification, but also about true glory? Surely when they come to the deification which I have mentioned, they stop in obvious shame, and truth drags them in its own direction despite their resistance. Does Livy explain this clearly enough in the introduction to his lengthy and famous work, where he undertook Roman history from the founding of the city itself, and fearing the judgment neither of the people nor of his own emperor, does he not simultaneously force both reverence and love for Romulus to yield to the truth? He said of Rome's founder, "We grant to antiquity this license, that it may make the origins of its cities more illustrious by mixing the human with the divine, and if any people are allowed to sanctify their origins and to exalt their founders to the gods, the Roman people have so much glory in war that when they exalt Mars, their ancestor and the parent of their founder, in preference to all others, the peoples of the world tolerate this with as much imperturbability as they tolerate the Roman Empire."[9]

Look how bright the truth is! A pagan man, one who extols the Roman name, ascribes no truth, not one whit, I say, to the divinity of Romulus. Instead, he attributes it to the indulgence of antiquity, the license of making their origins illustrious, and the tolerance of conquered nations. Therefore, there is nothing substantial, but it is all vacuous assumption and opinion.

In the last book of his *City of God,* St. Augustine understood that this is really what Livy had felt: "Who except Rome believed that Romulus was a god and, indeed, believed it only when the city itself was small and just beginning? Afterwards future generations had to preserve the traditions of their ancestors so that as the state grew and came to so much power, nursed as it were on the mother's milk of that superstition, it imposed this belief, as from a certain vantage point, on all the nations which it dominated, not so that they would believe that Romulus was a god, but so that they would nevertheless say so and not offend the state they served by giving its founder some other name than Rome did."[10]

Note what Livy confessed in his words cited above, where he says that the nations patiently endured the deification of Romulus just as they did the dominion of Rome itself. He who is constrained does not approve, but is unable or unwilling to oppose it. Indeed, Rome itself was still small, as St. Augustine says. Discussing the birth of Romulus and his brother with less reverence, he says, "When the raped Vestal Virgin had given birth to twin offspring, she vowed publicly that Mars was the father of her offspring of dubious origin, thinking that it was either true or more honorable to claim a god as the cause of her sin."[11] God, however, has never originated sin. Indeed, He is offended by nothing more than sin, and He always originates its opposite. So if this was the nature of Romulus' origin or of his life, which Livy, our source, does not assume is well-known to everyone, we can easily judge how strong that ladder must have been to elevate him to heaven by affection and praise.

What does that same Livy say about Aeneas, who men claim founded the Caesarian family and was deified as well? "The second battle with the Latins was also the last of Aeneas' mortal deeds. He was buried above the river Numicus. Whatever it is just and right to call him, they call him 'the deified hero of the land.'"[12] Even this is not the truth, but only the opinion of the common people. If Livy was sure about the location of the tomb, he had his doubts about Aeneas' posthumous title. No, he really did not doubt, but pretended that he did, and hesitating thus between the might of truth and Roman majesty, lest the one offend the other, he made a decision in this matter on the side of certain truth.

Come now, let us leave the philosophers and historians and hear what the poets think. Horace in his *Odes* says this openly: "What would Romulus, the son of Rhea Silvia and Mars, be if his merits were jealously kept in silence?"[13] What we still need to decide is whose glory is harmed by saying nothing and whose is benefited by the conversations of humanity. This is something which soon becomes increasingly obvious in his other poems when "Virtue, favor, and the tongue of powerful prophets deify Aeacus,[14] who was snatched from the waves of the Styx to immortality, and consecrate magnificent temples to him. The Muse forbids a man worthy of praise to die."[15]

Listen! I hear the tongue and the genius of poets hallowing and giving birth to immortality! What more is there? They were even responsible for that divinity which they worshipped in heaven, for he goes on to say, "The Muse rejoices in heaven."[16] This is exemplified in the story of Hercules, in those stories about the brothers [Castor and Pollux] born of Leda, and about the wine god Bacchus. He says that Hercules was present at the banquets of the gods, that Castor and Pollux brought aid to shipwrecked sailors, and that Bacchus led the prayers of mortals to their desired outcomes. All these sources agree that such stories arise from fame and poetic eloquence. It is not at all clear what sort of god lured into such sacrilegious error those very learned, knowledgeable, and prudent men who had been captivated by the glory of those people's names.

Lucan's words about the Caesars do not require explanation when he says, "Civil wars will make them divine and equal to the gods above. Rome will adorn their souls with lightning bolts, halos, and stars and will swear oaths through the shades in the temples of the gods."[17] Even after the race of the Caesars had been extinguished, we know that their name was preserved for many centuries afterward. Vergil, talking about the city of Rome and Caesar Augustus, also wrote this in his *Bucolics*: "Here every year at Meliboea I saw him as a young man, the same man to whom our altars smoke for twelve days at a time."[18] So great a man was not embarrassed to call Augustus a god and added in his raving: "For he will always be a god to me: a tender lamb from our sheep folds will forever offer its blood at his altar."[19] Consider how he asserts that a mortal, albeit a great man, is also a god and how he offers a sacrifice to him. The people's obsession with Augustus was so great that they bestowed on him during his life what had been bestowed and would be bestowed on all others after death, according to the poem of Horace: "While you are alive, we heap up divine offerings to you, and we set up altars for swearing vows in your name."[20]

My time would run out if I wanted to pursue all the testimonies of writers on this issue, but these citations are sufficient, and the rest can be deduced from them. I do not want to omit in my haste a comment made by that greatest philosopher, utmost genius, and peerless orator Marcus Cicero in his book, *On the Nature of the Gods.* I have taken this comment, however, from a source other than Cicero, to show that a pagan witness and a Christian witness could agree on something and think the same way, although they may have different opinions on other matters. In the same book in which he provided whatever weapons he could for our faith by disarming the errors of non-Christians, Lactantius, who was himself a great man and one of us, revealed the whole world of the gods with his marvelous and praiseworthy desire for knowledge and opened a path for St. Augustine and for others who followed him. After discussing many ideas about the original creation of gods, he added this: "Then, because the kings had been loved by those whose life they had ruled, they left behind a great longing for themselves when they died. Therefore, humans made statues so that they would gain some consolation from contemplating those images, and going even further in their love, they began to worship the memory of the deceased so much that they seemed to render thanks for their rulers' benefits and to encourage these kings' successors to want to rule well."[21] Strengthening his argument with these words as his testimony, he said, "This is what Cicero teaches about the nature of the gods when he says, 'This is the way of men and common custom: to raise to heaven with fame and affection those men who are distinguished by their good deeds: this is what happened to Hercules, Castor and Pollux, Bacchus, and Aesculapius, the god of healing.'[22] Elsewhere he says, 'In several states the memory of powerful men, consecrated by the honor of being raised to the level of immortal gods, was understandably used either to exalt virtue or to encourage the best men to risk death for the state more willingly.'[23]

"It was evidently with this in mind that Roman Caesars and Moors deified their own kings. Superstitions thus gradually took shape when the people who had first known them passed that ritual on to their children and grandchildren, then to all their descendants. Hence, these great kings were worshipped in all the provinces because of the fame of their name.

"Especially, however, individual populations paid the highest veneration to the founders of their own tribe or city: men outstanding in bravery or women noteworthy for their chastity. Egypt worshipped Isis; the Moors, Juba; the Macedonians, Cabyrus; the Carthaginians, Urania; the Latins, Faunus; the Sabines, Sacus; and the Romans, Quirinus. In the same way, Athens worshipped Minerva; Samos worshipped Juno; Paphos, Venus; Lemnos, Vulcan; Naxos, Bacchus[24]; and Delos, Apollo. Thus different rites were begun among their own populations and regions because people wished to show gratitude to their leaders and were unable to find any other honors to offer them after they died.

"In addition, the devotion of those who followed them added a good deal to this error. So that their heroes might seem to have been born from divine ancestry, those people offered divine honors to their ancestors and ordered divine honors to be offered by others. Can anyone doubt how the superstitions about the gods arose when he reads in Vergil the words of Aeneas, who told his comrades: 'Offer now libation saucers to Jupiter and call on my father Anchises in prayer.'[25] Aeneas attributed to his father not only immortality, but also power over the winds: 'Let us request the winds and say that these sacred rites of mine will be offered to him in temples for as many years as he wishes after our city has been established.'[26]

"The descendants of Jupiter, Bacchus, Pan, Mercury, and Apollo did the same thing, and later their successors did the same thing for them. Poets even came forth and extolled them to heaven in the poems which they composed for their delight, just as those people do who use panegyrics of dubious veracity to praise kings, even those kings who are evil. What evil sprang from the Greeks, whose shallowness arose from their skill in speaking? It is incredible what great clouds of lies this crowd stirred up. Therefore, admiring those gods, they first began the worship of them and passed it on to all nations. Because of this deception the Sibyl scolded them in Greek thus: 'O Greece, why do you trust human beings to be your guides? Why do you bring useless gifts to the dead? Why do you pile up sacrificial animals for idols? Who has planted this error in your mind that you would do these things and abandon the face of the great God.'"[27]

To these citations we may add what we read in the book of Wisdom: "The rare skill of an artist contributed to the worship of these men and those they did not know because, wanting to please the ruler who had hired him, the artist worked with skill so that the likeness [of the ruler] would become more beautiful. The multitude, attracted by the charm of his work, now regarded that person, whom shortly before they had honored as a man, as an object of worship. This was a deception about the nature of human life because men, bound by affection or royal authority, bestowed on objects of stone or wood a name that ought not to be shared."[28] Obviously what he says about "affection" and "royal authority" pertains to what Cicero has assigned as the basis of the error, that is, reverence for outstanding men, and to Lactantius' "reverence for dead kings." Lactantius, however, adds both respect and the feelings for one's ancestors as reasons: each seems to me to be a possible motive.

Therefore, according to Cicero, it is correct that the poets constructed by exaggeration, or as Lactantius says, that illustrious artists, painters, or sculptors did so, because there is nothing more useful than the arts for creating errors. Artisans charm the eyes; poets charm the ears. It is precisely by these senses that truth enters the soul. Moreover, after explaining these matters which you have just heard, Lactantius returns to Cicero: "Marcus Tullius was not only an accomplished orator, but also a philosopher, a single great imitator of Plato in that book in which he consoled himself for the death of his daughter. He did not hesitate to say that gods who were being worshipped had once been human beings. This testimonial of Cicero himself ought to be judged very seriously because he held the priestly post of 'augur'[29] and testified that he worshipped and venerated these gods. So within a few lines he has told us two things, for when he tells us that he is going to dedicate a statue of his daughter in the same way as the ancients dedicated their images of gods, he has both taught us that those people were dead and has shown us the origin of an empty superstition. He says, 'We truly see that so many people, both men and women, have been deified by humans, and when we worship their august shrines in cities and in the countryside, let us approve of their wisdom because our whole lives are set up and arranged by their genius and by their ideas of laws and institutions. If any living creature, however, had to be worshipped, it was surely my daughter Tullia. If the progeny of Cadmus, Amphitryon, or Tindareus[30] had to be deified because of their fame, the same honor ought to be decreed to my daughter. Indeed, I will do this, and with the approval of the immortal gods I will consecrate you, the best and the most learned of all, and will place you in their company for the respect of all mortals.'"[31]

These are certainly the words of Cicero to the letter, in which he held to his principle and expressed his grief in such a way as not to contradict the truth as wise men consider it. At the same time he recalled that people were usually exalted to heaven, not by any truth, but by their excellence. Following the example of those who had preceded him, he promised that he would worship his dead daughter, whom he had loved with the utmost devotion, and that he would place her in the council of gods because of her excellence and education, not truly, but in the opinion of all mortals, with the additional approval of those "gods" who are delighted by nothing more than the mistakes and superstitions of mortals. We can easily believe that whether they were bad men or demons, these "gods" voluntarily agreed with Cicero in the deification of his daughter because, whether he spoke in error or knowingly, the eloquence of Cicero would at least give rise to error in the minds of those whose weaker intelligence would be dulled by his splendid words.

Of course, when Lactantius was discussing with some concern this very point of Cicero's, he said, "Perhaps someone may say that Cicero was delirious from too much grief, yet that whole treatise, as far as erudition, examples, and his perfect manner of speaking are concerned, was not the work of a sick mind, but a constant mind and judgment, and his presentation itself reflects no trace of grief. Nor do I think that he could write so fluently on such varied matters unless reason itself, the consolation of his friends, and the passage of time had softened his grief."[32] The diligent reader will understand how true Lactantius' conjecture was, not so much from this source as from Cicero's own letters to Atticus.[33] To eliminate all suspicion about Cicero's book, *Consolation,* which doubtless was written under the influence of grief, Lactantius uses the testimony of Cicero's other illustrious tomes and says, "What of the fact that Cicero says the same thing in his books *On the State* and *On Glory*? Following the ideas of Plato in that work *On the Laws,* Cicero wanted to propose laws which he thought a just and wise state would use. Thus he decreed concerning religion: 'They shall worship the gods, those who have always been considered divine beings, and those whose deserving actions have placed them in heaven to be worshipped, such as Hercules, Bacchus, Aesculapius, Castor, Pollux, and Quirinus [the deified Romulus].'"[34]

Here, it seems to me, he speaks more ambiguously than usual so he can suggest that certain figures were always heavenly and almost native-born and that others were like parvenus placed in heaven, not by nature, but by the consensus of humanity. Maybe he was saying that the former had not always been divine in fact, but just in the human mind, that is, that they had been deified in common opinion, and that the only difference was that some were believed to be gods from some nebulous point in time, others from eternity. He said this more openly in his *Tusculan Disputations.* Maybe he feared that the people would hate someone who wrote seemingly useless laws for the republic or who destroyed popular beliefs. Therefore, he concealed his thoughts in his legal books, which were addressed to the people, and spoke more clearly in his philosophical works, where he addressed educated men.

Even there, however, Lactantius perceived that Cicero was afraid, for Lactantius speaks this way: "When Cicero in his *Tusculan Disputations* said that all of heaven was almost filled with the human race, he said, 'If I should try to examine the old books and to reach some conclusion from the words which Greek writers have revealed, those gods of the greater nations are considered to have started out from here, from among us, into the heavens. Seek those whose tombs are pointed out in Greece. Because you have been initiated, remember the knowledge that is handed down in the mysteries. You will finally understand how widely this is known.'"[35] Therefore, I certainly recognize no fear in these words of Cicero. He even confesses frankly that even "major gods" left earth for the heavens, but everyone ought to understand this one basic fact: these gods did not really arrive there, but people believed that they had.

What could be clearer than this confession? What is the source, I wonder, of what Lactantius says here: "He appealed to the knowledge of Atticus,"[36] although he might better have said "of Brutus," for it is to Brutus, not to Atticus, that he addressed the book *Tusculan Disputations,* but this is not very important. Let us only pay attention to what he affirmed: "He argued that we can understand from the mysteries themselves that all those who are worshipped have actually been human beings."[37] Lactantius is certainly right about this in Cicero's case, but what sort of comment follows? He says: "And when he confessed without hesitation regarding Hercules, Bacchus, Aesculapius, Castor, and Pollux, he was afraid to admit this openly about their fathers Jupiter and Apollo, likewise about Neptune, Vulcan, Mars, and Mercury, whom he called the gods of the greater generations. Therefore, he says that this is common knowledge, that we should understand the same thing about Jupiter and the other more ancient gods. If our ancestors worshipped their memory in the same way that he says he will worship the image and name of his daughter, they can be forgiven for their grieving, but not for their belief in those gods. Who can be so lacking in judgment as to think that heaven is open to the dead at the consent and pleasure of countless stupid people, or that someone could give to another what he himself does not have?"[38]

While I confess that these words were spoken with divine inspiration, I certainly do not think that Cicero was afraid to speak out. If he could call on his friend's recollection to swear that one could understand from the mysteries how widespread was the knowledge of what he had said, he wished that what was said about less important gods should also be applied to the "major gods." However, he himself had said that very thing expressly, namely that the "major gods" were found to have gone to heaven, starting from here on earth. As the basis of this affirmation he cites the traditional mysteries to which he directed his friend's mind and memory. Indeed, if Christian writers did not insist as they do, and if pagan writers did not believe on their own that individual issues pertinent to their religion were meaningless and irrelevant to them, nevertheless, it was enough for all intelligent people that the pagan writers say that the earth is the mother of all the gods and also of all humanity. Thus, according to Cicero, all the gods of all peoples, no matter what their superstition, sanctioned by however many years, are to be worshipped and must continue to be worshipped as earth-bound and mortal men, not as gods.

If this error of theirs had stayed within limits, there would be only the great danger of attributing to humans what was owed to God. Devils, however, relying on this opportunity, entered the statues of the dead with innate cleverness, and taking advantage of our credulity and inexperience, they gave rise to a double source of trouble. If one offers divine homage not only to a human, but also to a devil who is the enemy of God, through a mere statue whose body is material and whose soul is a demon and the deceiver of humanity (and in this way created out of a body and soul made by a human), is it any wonder that he becomes a "god"? Trimegistus says that humanity was given the devil's artifice for doing this,[39] and he complains that it was either taken away at the arrival of the true God or ought to be taken away.

This is the conclusion: those clever people of antiquity were fooled either by the vain memory of dead men living in the underworld or by the lies and statues of devils. The result was the unbelievable hardship that beset them as a worthy punishment. Indeed, I confess that it would never have occurred to me that in my attempt to show that gods were created by humans, I would introduce into my text so many lines from Lactantius and Cicero, except for the fact that I remembered that those books, from which I draw my citations, are otherwise rare and most likely not available to you. Therefore because you have the book of Wisdom at your fingertips, I willingly and knowingly have omitted those things which I knew were similarly written in that book about the origin of idols and superstitions.

The citations agree with Ciceronian opinion so much that Cicero can be believed to have adapted them from Philo, or (more in accordance with chronology) that Philo adapted them from Cicero. Perhaps after you examine the ways of each of them, neither one seems to have read the writings of the other, but rather to have gone together down the same path because of a certain equality of genius without realizing how much they agreed, especially because Aristotle's statement is true, that "everything is in harmony."[40]

❧   ❧   ❧

NOTES

1. Ps. 45:11.
2. Ps. 83:8.
3. Graeco-Roman demigods who legend says rallied the Romans to victory at a battle against the Latins at Lake Regillus in 494 B.C.E.
4. Cicero, *Against Catiline* 3.1.
5. Cf. Ovid, *Fasti* 2.491-512.
6. Lucan, *Pharsalia* 1.197.
7. Cicero, *On Duties* 3.41.
8. Quirinus is Romulus' name as a god.
9. Livy, *From the Founding of the City*, Preface 7.
10. Augustine, *City of God* 22.6.
11. Livy, *From the Founding of the City* 1.4.2.
12. Op. cit., 1.2.6.
13. Horace, *Odes* 4.8.22-24.

14. Aeacus, the son of Zeus and Europa, was the brother of King Minos of Crete.

15. Horace, *Odes* 4.8.25-28.

16. Ibid.

17. Lucan, *Pharsalia* 7.457-59.

18. Vergil, *Bucolics (Eclogues)* 1.42-43.

19. Ibid., 1.7-8.

20. Horace, *Epistles* 2.1.15-16.

21. Lactantius, *Divine Institutions* 1.15.3-4.

22. Lactantius quotes from Cicero, *On the Nature of the Gods* 2.24.62.

23. *On the Nature of the Gods* 3.19.50. Lactantius seems to be quoting Cicero through the last paragraph on page 120.

24. Petrarch's mythology confuses Greek and Roman names. Greek cities and islands obviously worshipped Athena, Hera, Aphrodite, Hephaestus, and Dionysus, respectively. Apollo is Apollo in both cultures.

25. Vergil, *Aeneid* 7.133-34.

26. Ibid., 5.59-60.

27. Lactantius, *Divine Institutions.*

28. Wisd. 14:18-21.

29. A Roman augur observed the motions and actions of birds to predict whether or not the omens were favorable for an important undertaking.

30. Cadmus was the grandfather of Bacchus; Amphitryon, the mortal father of Hercules; Tindareus, the mortal father of Castor and Pollux.

31. Lactantius, *Divine Institutions* 1.15.16-20, from Cicero, *Consolation,* fragment 11.

32. Lactantius, *Divine Institutions* 1.15.21-22.

33. Cf. Cicero, *To Atticus* 12.14. Cicero's best friend, Atticus, spent most of his adult life in Greece.

34. Lactantius, *Divine Institutions* 1.15.23, from Cicero, *On the Laws* 2.19.

35. Lactantius, *Divine Institutions* 1.15.24, from Cicero, *Tusculan Disputations* 1.29.

36. Lactantius, *Divine Institutions* 1.15.26.

37. Ibid.

38. Ibid.

39. Hermes Trimegistus, *Asclepius* 37.

40. Aristotle, *Nicomachean Ethics* 1098b.11.

5

We must reject all the paths by which those people who have descended to hell were believed to have climbed into heaven, for they are not paths, but certainly dead-end roads. They do not lead where we are headed. Who can show us the right path? We have to stay as far as possible from deserts and swamps. Indeed, we must make our way along a high and difficult hill. We have to abandon vice and seize upon virtue, desert stupidity, and follow wisdom, for the end of the former is usually the beginning of the latter. This we can see in the words of Horace: "It is virtue to flee vice, and wisdom begins when we give up our follies."[1] Illustriously indeed the satirist Juvenal says, "Surely the only peaceful path of life begins with virtue."[2] Indeed, it is the only peaceful path of life, nor do we seek any other way. We seek the path of life that leads through virtue, for it leads nowhere else but where we want to go.

What does the Psalmist say? "They will go from virtue unto virtue."[3] This is the path, and this end which follows: "The God of gods will be seen on Zion."[4] So the way to this sight is through virtue. O what a glorious journey! O what a blessed goal! I ask, how often have we who live here on earth set off to some pleasant dwelling place to see a friend's longed-for face? We eagerly walk along a path through shady valleys and dewy meadows, through leafy and low hills, along the pleasant and flowery banks of rivers, and in the meanwhile, forgetting the labors of the road, we soothe our eyes with the sights we encounter. How much more pleasant is this path? How much more blessed is this goal: to go through this short life, brief as a winter's day, taking the high and delightful path, the easy one once you have become accustomed to it, and climbing from virtue to virtue, so that by nightfall you will see the highest and most blessed God of gods on Zion. Unless I am totally mistaken, this is our true end, for as St. Augustine wrote in the last chapter of *The City of God*, "What else is our goal except to reach the kingdom which has no end?"[5]

Friendship and virtue are undoubtedly the sweetest of blessings in this life. What enjoyment of them (or of virtually any other blessing, real or imaginable) is as great as reaching that ultimate point, that most peaceful source of all delight and joy when one "will be drunk on the fullness of the house of God and will drink from the swift stream of His pleasure? Truly in His presence is the source of life, and in His light we will see the light."[6] Therefore I am amazed at how blind some people can be:

because they are very greedy for pleasure and seek it with all their effort. Thus it often happens that some minor pleasure pulls them away from that highest pleasure, but desire for pleasure ought to have caused them, who up to this point were delighted by small pleasures, to seek that one and highest pleasure.

If a grassy field and a tiny fountain under the shade of a tree is so attractive to a tired traveler, what is it like to have discovered among the troubles of mortal life "a fountain of water which springs up into eternal life"[7] and that shade under which we may be protected from the heat of the sun and from all adversity and from all fear, not just for the space of a brief hour, but forever? If it is sweet to see and to talk about the shining ray of the sun, sunny lands, flowering branches, and green meadows, or gold wiped and polished by a master artisan's hand, or shining gems washed up on the shore of India, or (the best of all) the face of a dear friend, what sort of sight will there be when we behold what everyone realizes is the source from which all this pleasure springs? Whatever delights our eyes or ears, our senses and our mind, how, pray tell, could it delight us if it did not come from that Source which not only towers over all delights, but even created them and has given to them the ability, not only to delight us, but even to exist? This is why I think that in all its affairs humanity has no equivalent madness, no insanity so common, as being distracted by some tiny, uncertain, and brief pleasure and thus being turned away from that immense, sure, and eternal joy, without which this temporal pleasure would be nothing. Furthermore, I do not satisfactorily understand the reason for this evil which so easily distracts us, unless it is the custom of human diffidence to love what is present and to scorn what is in the future, even though the blessing of divine love, being greater and better, can be more certain and more present than the blessing of human love. In many matters, especially in those which deal with carnal desires, hope may be considerably sweeter than reality itself.

But the fickleness of human minds is such that it is difficult to define what they want for themselves and what they do not want, not only in all other matters, but especially in this one, because they simultaneously seek and flee that pleasure in which they set up the greatest good. There is nothing wrong with this, provided that they can distinguish between true and false pleasure. So much for this.

What merited thanks will you pay to God, my brothers, Who has revealed to you in your humility,[8] just as He would to little children, what has been kept hidden from so many proud and wise men, namely what the soul's path truly is, what goal of life and what leader you have? Many wise men have vigorously debated the goals of good and bad men. Marcus Tullius Cicero, that chief exemplar of Roman eloquence, whom St. Augustine names one of the most learned and eloquent of all men, devoted an entire volume divided into five books to this subject. Moreover, Marcus Varro, Cicero's contemporary and scholarly companion, considered the same question so scrupulously and so minutely in his book *On Philosophy*, as St. Augustine recalls,[9] that by some subtle hairsplitting of distinctions, he broke philosophy down into 288 divisions which either had already arisen or could arise from these sources of opinion. Among these sects there is a complex and unresolved dispute about this very goal which we are seeking.

I pass over these matters as well, for they are well known, and I consciously pass by those three more famous schools of thought. Who has not heard how Epicurus establishes pleasure as the utmost good? Both we and the philosophers of this world reject that opinion, although the rest of the world seems to follow only this goal and to assert it in the way it comports itself. The Peripatetics say that virtue is the utmost good, and the Stoics say that it is the only good. Thus, both have almost the same goal. How far can one go beyond the "highest" or the "only" good? One should stop when one has nowhere else to go or nowhere to stop. There, assuredly, is the goal of life.

Furthermore, who is ignorant of those three paths on which the whole human race walks: the path of desire, the path of civic duty, and the path of contemplation? Aristotle discusses this in his *Ethics*.[10] Many poets discuss these goals under the nebulous disguise of mythology in that dispute among the three goddesses.[11] When a knowledgeable, but evidently corruptible, judge was chosen to decide the quarrel, he preferred Venus and the life of love to the other two, as do all men who are inclined to the choice of a bestial life because of the weakening of their senses or the passions of their mind.

In all these sects, nevertheless, and in others, if they exist, there is no (or very rarely any) mention of God among those philosophers. Although some reach pleasure, others attain something else, and those who rise higher reach virtue. There their philosophical quest stops and rests as if it has reached its goal, but the more enduring light of Truth has appeared to us, not through our own merit, but by divine gift, so we begin where those philosophers cease, for we do not strive toward virtue as an end unto itself, but we strive toward God through virtues. Thus it has been written: "They will go from virtue unto virtue; the God of gods will be seen on Zion."[12] Virtue is the path; God is the goal seen on Zion. We have learned from the testimony of Holy Scriptures that Zion was a "sacred mountain,"[13] thus we should know that we need an elevated mind and high and holy thoughts to reach this blessed vision. Therefore, although the illustrious philosophers of all nations relate everything to virtue, the philosopher of Christ relates virtue itself to God, the Creator of virtue. Using virtues, he enjoys God and never lets his mind stop short of that goal. He hears a certain great philosopher of Christ saying, "You have established us for Yourself, and for this reason our heart shall be restless until it finds peace in You."[14] I will not leave Epicurus unmentioned. If Aristotle, Plato, Cicero, or Seneca (whichever of the four was the most honest), the Epicureans and Cynics, and whatever other writers there have been whose beliefs are damned, were asked about the goal of good works or the greatest blessing, all would either hesitate in responding or would merely disagree with the others. What Christian anywhere is so simple and uneducated, provided that he is a true Christian, that he would have doubts about the goals of good and evil men, that he would not resolutely declare, as Augustine himself did, that "the greatest blessing is eternal life, and eternal death the greatest evil"[15]? If "this is eternal life, that they should know that You alone are the true God and Jesus Christ Whom You sent,"[16] let each one judge for himself what eternal death is.

These are humanity's goals, one of which we must embrace as eagerly as we can, provided the same God who has taught us those things will give us a hand, lift us up, and help our feebleness. We must studiously reject the other goal as the worst possibility there is. Christ does not stand in the way because Christ calls Himself the "Way."[17] In the same passage He calls Himself the "Life." Severinus Boethius speaks the truth: "He is the Leader, the Path, and the End all in One."[18]

O great philosophers and hard-working men whose natural intelligence overwhelms us, look at how we have overtaken you in grace and free blessings. You have labored, but look at how we now rest. You have planted, but look at how we now harvest. You have sought, but look at how we now find. It is neither your fault nor our merit, but only the favor of God which has done this, "Who loved Jacob, but held Esau in hatred."[19] While He showed you many mysteries and the causes of many things, He kept Himself hidden as the highest and the best. Why did it happen that you philosophers, being unable to see any higher, placed "good" only in virtue? Did you think that you had reached your goal, miserably surrounded by shadows? Did you lie down on the road and dare to promise yourself happiness in a place that was an abode of labor and misery? Some of you thought that a person could become happy solely through virtue; others thought that this could happen through the acquisition of many trifling and impermanent possessions. What a short-lived and absurd sort of "happiness"! What a meaningless definition of educated men! What folly it is to put an iced dessert in the fire, to put life in the middle of death, and to call a traveler blessed amidst so many dead ends, so many steep and ragged climbs, so many slippery places, amidst so many ambushes by bandits, when he is convinced of danger and toil, doubtful of rest, and unsure of being welcomed anywhere. Will anyone, exposed to so many misfortunes and ignorant of his lot in life, dare to call himself blessed just because he sometimes seems to progress according to mortal virtue, but does not know where his journey may take him or where it may end? That is similar to saying that anyone who starts a pleasant journey and is also sure about his destination can be happy, or as if the path, not the goal, can satisfy the traveler. Surely the most learned of your flock, philosophers as well as poets, feel that we have to wait for the final day of life for anyone to be called blessed and that nobody living can ever be blessed according to this idea.[20]

Nevertheless, they themselves dream of some sort of blessedness, I know not why. At odds with themselves, they call life both happy and miserable at the same time. Armed with their wits, they defend and protect their circumlocutions with meticulously considered conclusions. I believe that if they turn their eyes to themselves and to the course of their life, they will understand that they are recalling things which are specious rather than true. Moreover, our Lord Christ has shown us this path of miseries and that we must seek happiness elsewhere. I do not describe the tribulations of mortals: would that they were not so well-known to all of us! Cicero, however, explained them as best he could in his *Consolation*, and after him St. Augustine did the same, but more carefully, in the last book of *The City of God*.[21]

To prove my point briefly, but effectively, I touch upon that which Apuleius, that great follower of Plato, wrote in his book *The God of*

Socrates. Speaking about himself and about us, who lead this miserable and trouble-ridden life, he said, "Confiding in reason and acquiring strength from their speech, with souls that are immortal and limbs that are destined to die, with fickle and worrying minds, dull and foul bodies, very different customs, very similar flaws; marked by stubborn audacity, precarious hope, unfruitful labor, and fleeting fortune, human beings are mortal as individuals, but immortal as part of the human race. Individuals disappear in turn, leaving only enough offspring to take their place, inhabiting the earth for only a moment of time, and complaining about everything. Humans are slow in obtaining wisdom, but quick in death."[22]

Is there someone who loves this life so much that he thinks these words of mine characterize the happy man? As far as I am concerned, not at all. They seem to describe wandering animals and to be as far as possible from the very happiness which we are seeking. When I think about the tortures of a laborious and anxious life, I consider that this man [Apuleius] has drawn these words from the source of truth and nature, and how I wish he were mistaken! But certainly he is not.

How much more vehemently do I wonder at the audacity of those who dare to claim that something is their own when this life's current is so rapid, so precarious, and so uncertain. Death and unhappiness are always at the door despite their presumption of a happy life. Surely in their human eagerness they believed that virtue was to be sought by human effort, that happiness came from virtue and other things which are connected with virtue. For this reason they left no role for God in the affairs of humanity. Aristotle himself, however, after saying "What therefore keeps us from calling 'happy' a person who lives according to perfect virtue and sufficiently endowed by external goods?"[23] and other words with which he struggled to construct happiness like some building of wood, stone, and lime, soon adds, "We will call 'happy' those of the living who possess or will possess those properties of which we have spoken."[24] Finally he added one thing which seems to me to have tempered this philosophical insolence somewhat. He says "happy, however, as human beings,"[25] as if to say: I call them happy this way while remembering that they are human beings. What else does this mean, I ask, except that he calls those people happy who he knows are miserable? Thus all that philosophy which proposes so much laborious endeavor comes down to a joke. Sharpen your wits, gather your sophisms, turn the matter anyway you will: there is no happiness in mortal life except in either error or hope.

The first of these, error, is the utmost misery; the second is still an incomplete happiness because it cannot keep its footing on this sloping path. I think that if those who dispute this would put aside their zeal for arguing, as I have said, and look inside themselves or just look around, they will admit, even if only tacitly, that I am speaking the truth and that they are defending falsehood, albeit cleverly. Perhaps they may assert that the Roman general Metellus,[26] whom I have mentioned previously, and Sophidius, that penniless farmer of Arcadia, were happy. Valerius Maximus seems to have found those two alone of the whole human race to be worthy of the false designation of happiness.[27] I wish they could both be here so I could interrogate them face to face. By Hercules, I believe that in disagreement with the historian, they would call themselves just as happy as Valerius was truthful in this regard, nor was the oracle Apollo more truthful than Valerius, who replied that Sophidius himself was happier than the king of the Lydians, unless a less miserable man is sometimes said to be happier in comparison to even greater misery. Certainly Pliny the Elder, a man of great intelligence and voluminous learning, says that this Sophidius, the cultivator of a small farm "which he never left," was not so much happy, but "experienced very little evil in his life because of limited desires."[28] Who does not see how great a gulf lies between the least evil and that greatest and supreme good which encompasses happiness? Therefore, the man whom Valerius had classified as happy, Pliny classifies as less miserable and uses many weighty arguments to prove that Metellus himself and, even more amazingly, Augustus Caesar were not happy.[29]

Lest I get mired in individual examples, Pliny produces a limited and brief statement about Sophidius, in which Pliny proves not to be a sophist, as most of them were, but an accomplished philosopher. He says, "If we wish to judge fairly and make a decision placing no hope in fortune, we would admit that no mortal is happy."[30]

Listen to me, you who make one of your kind happy as you would a small vessel which you yourself made; even if this man can perhaps be imagined, this great man says that he can never be found among mortals and then added, "He lives fully and is indulgently blessed by fortune who can truly be called not unhappy."[31] I will not consider what he adds to these words, for although they are many and valid, nevertheless, there are infinite, unassailable reasons that reinforce and defend this truth, all of which I pass over in silence lest I dwell too long on this very obvious fact. I think that the unspoken testimony of the individual conscience suffices. Let each person study them for himself in the innermost recesses of his heart and his conscience: whoever considers himself happy, let him protest that I have lied. Indeed, I hope that I will be guilty of lying in a few cases. Whatever quantity of pleasant things may be imagined, whatever prosperity of fortune, whatever peace of mind, it will not be that happiness which we seek.

We surely lack that one thing that assures us that we lack nothing. Without it everything else is nothing. The abundance of all earthly things belongs to exiles: the condition of our earthbound exile diminishes all the pleasure of enticing fortune. We are now truly living in exile from our everlasting home and "wandering away from God and cast forth from His face and eyes."[32] What happiness do we seek, of what joy do we dream? "We sit by the rivers of Babylon and weep if we remember you, O Zion, and hang our harps in the bitter willow trees."[33]

If, however, we have even forgotten Zion, how much more miserable is our exile because we have lost that memory which by itself was powerful enough to take us back to our homeland, lessen our misery, and even render us happy sometimes? Therefore, in my opinion, when people excuse the ancients who defined happiness as something to be found here on earth, on the grounds that they remembered neither their homeland nor their Lord, they certainly do not excuse their ignorance, but increase their misery. Can anything be more miserable than to be so miserable that we not only forget that we are miserable, but also consider ourselves happy besides?

❧   ❧   ❧

NOTES

1. Horace, *Epistles* 1.1.41-42.
2. Juvenal, *Satires* 10.363-64.
3. Ps. 83:8.
4. Ibid.
5. Augustine, *City of God* 22.30.
6. Ps. 35:9-10.
7. John 4:14.
8. Cf. Luke 10:21.
9. Augustine, *City of God* 19.1.
10. Aristotle, *Nicomachean Ethics* 1095b.14–1096a.10.
11. The judgment of Paris prior to the Trojan War, deciding whether Juno, Minerva, or Venus were the fairest.
12. Ps. 83:8.
13. Ps. 2:6, Joel 3:17.
14. Augustine, *Confessions* 1.1.
15. Augustine, *City of God* 19.4.
16. John 17:3.
17. John. 14:6.
18. Boethius, *Consolation of Philosophy* 3, metr. 9.28. Severinus Boethius (480–524) was a Roman senator and one of the last great minds of the late Roman period.
19. Rom. 9:13.
20. Cf. Aristotle, *Nicomachean Ethics* 1100a.32-34.
21. Augustine, *City of God* 22.22.
22. Apuleius, *The God of Socrates* 4.
23. Aristotle, *Nicomachean Ethics* 1101a.14-21.
24. Ibid.
25. Ibid.
26. For Metellus, see above, p. 32 n. 32.
27. Valerius Maximus, 7.1.1-2.
28. Pliny, *Natural History* 7.46.151.
29. Cf. Pliny, *Natural History* 7.44-45.

30. Ibid. 7.40.130.
31. Ibid.
32. 2 Cor. 5:6, Ps. 30:23.
33. Ps. 136:1-2.

6

So enough discussion about false happiness. What should I say about virtue, which philosophers claim to be the foundation of that happiness? They are not mistaken as long as they acknowledge the Architect and Crown of that foundation. Of course, philosophers attribute to human effort self-restraint and those other virtues which are actually the gift of God. They believe habit is created by repeating acts, as if either one act of virtue or the choice itself were within the power of humanity without the help of God. Yet there is no mention among them of His assistance. Rare indeed is the mention of God Himself among them, as I have said.

One feels shame and pity for human pride. What can I say except that such pride deserves to be punished forcibly and without restraint? Can anyone become chaste, just, holy, and innocent by himself and without effort, just because he wishes to? Philosophers will all respond unanimously: he surely cannot do this without effort, as they say, but he can by mental concentration and determination. Once we have fixed our attention on this end, what can keep us from becoming good? Doubtlessly nothing except proud ingratitude and ungrateful pride. Nothing can keep a person from becoming good if he seeks this goal from the proper source and in the proper way. Otherwise, every attempt will be to no avail. Some cautious men, however, do not see this and usurp the job of the eternal King, and although they take great care to avoid the wrath of an earthly king and the crime of treason, they do not fear to commit unpardonable sacrilege against that King Who is our eternal and heavenly Majesty. So that there may be no lack of various sources of authority for their madness, they even have a poet who sounds like a philosopher, who not only does not demand the help of God for good qualities of the mind, but also excludes it as superfluous, although he does not deny that it is necessary in other matters. Horace says in his *Epistles:* "But it is enough to ask god, who gives and takes away, to give us life and riches: I will prepare for myself a calm mind."[1] So, Horace, you will prepare a calm mind for yourself? This may perhaps be part of your temerity: that you hope. You will never have the power to fulfill that hope. Therefore, because you think that a person should seek from God the least important of things, such as life, wealth, and those things which fortune gives to the worst and vilest men, do you think that you will achieve a contented mind without God? Humanity has nothing greater or better than a calm mind, and only a very good person is able to obtain it, but you have completely "missed the boat," as they say, to attribute small matters to God and great ones to yourself. You come closer to the mark elsewhere. Although afflicted by misfortune, you prayed to a god, but not to the One to Whom you should have, to grant you not only the opportunity to enjoy what you already had, which only fortune can dictate, but also good health in mind and body and an honorable old age lacking neither intellect nor eloquence.[2] In this respect you have done the right thing: these individual gifts must rightly be sought from heaven; they are not so much a matter of our own will as they are a gift of God.

This was said very well by that wise Christian writer St. Paul, who was surely more humble and more cautious and who confessed that self-control had to be sought from God, knowing that he could not acquire it any other way, just as he could acquire neither other virtues nor anything good at all. He wrote, "What do you have that you have not received?"[3]

Pre-Christian philosophers, however, either hold those things in low esteem or are ignorant of them, and as if they have never experienced how insubstantial human power is concerning even the smallest things, they conceive magnificent hopes for themselves and very lofty thoughts about their own possessions, and when they have fooled themselves by such thinking, they are eager to fool others by their arguments, and of course they trust in their skills and intelligence [and with respect to such things, do not ask who that man was about whom Persius spoke].[4] What very literate and learned men! How much they still must learn about the most important and dangerous matters!

Saint Augustine was speaking about such men when he said, "humanity is rich in human knowledge, but lacks divine knowledge. Not aware enough of their own strength, they invent stories to support their beliefs."[5] Elsewhere he says about them, "They do not philosophize at sacred moments, nor do they speak religiously in their philosophy."[6] Indeed, unless I am wrong, the zealotry and excitement of an argument arouse such people, but the desire to seek the truth does not move them. So you assume the false name of philosophy, and to you Aristotle is great, Plato is majestic, and the name of Christ is lowly and humble. You consider truth of little value unless it was reached through syllogisms, but truth is sought and found nowhere better than in silence.

Therefore, I say that according to these standards, it is consistent with your nature to attribute to yourselves those things which are God's. I tell you that this perverse idea and similar opinions have arisen from this forgetfulness of our own weakness. Why is it strange that those who believe that God doesn't care about mortal affairs hope that everything may come from themselves? Cicero spoke from this same source of self-confidence (lest I call it a source of insolence) in his *Tusculan Disputations:* "Death is encountered with the calmest mind at that point when a departing life can console itself with its own merits."[7] He has expressed the same sentiment elsewhere in other words, for he said, "Death is terrible for people whose possessions all come to an end with the end of their life, but not for those whose merit cannot die."[8] Mighty Cicero, what are you saying? What are you hoping? Whose life has ever been full of so much merit that if he did not look away and extol himself even higher, he could console himself with his own merit and not be tortured by the memory of his own wrongs? Besides, look at what you said: "with its own merits." What merit has ever belonged to man and not to God, whence comes not only the reason for which we earn merit, but also the very reason that we exist? I ask you: what is the glory of humanity? What is glory except that which you have learned from David (and I wish that you had learned it from Saint Paul): "My soul will be extolled in the Lord,"[9] and my merit is in God, and "He who would rejoice will rejoice in the Lord."[10] In the end, this is our glory, the testimony of our conscience. See, therefore, what you attribute to mortal man, whom you teach to console himself with a life of glory so that death may somehow be endured with a calm mind. I understand neither what these merits can be nor how a dying life can console itself except by that very Grace with which our sins are erased.

When our Ambrose lay dying and was ready to give up the ghost, his friends, who were weeping and fearing the destruction of Italy as a result of the death of such a great man, asked him to beg God for a longer life. He did not consent, but rather responded correctly, soberly, and better than all the philosophers, when he told them, "Because we have a good Master, I have not lived among you in such a way that I am ashamed to stay alive, nor do I fear to die."[11] This holy man is certainly a wise and true philosopher of Christ, for he assuaged his fear of death, not by his own praises, but by the goodness and grace of God, and he put his hope not in his own merits, but in the good Lord.

Now let Cicero step forth and console himself from his own philosophy, if he can, on that very day that he died near Gaeta. Ambrose nourished consolation and faith for himself by looking to Another, for he did not refer those words ("I have not lived in such a way among you that I am ashamed to stay alive") to the strict scrutiny of his merits under an infallible Judge, before Whom nobody, not even a day-old infant, is free from sin, as has been written. Rather, he referred them to the opinions of the people with whom he had lived, who are unable to make judgments about the life within us which they do not see. Had the time come to discuss the matter, he would have said that he placed his confidence, not in the fact that he had lived as he had, but in the fact that he had a good and kind Master. This is how the reply of Ambrose was understood by St. Augustine, who lived as the former's friend and fellow son of Christ. Having survived that man of God, he is said to have often recalled Ambrose's last words, which I have just stated, and praised them highly, admiring in these words, not the ornateness of a polished presentation, but the seriousness of his statement. This has been written in the biography of St. Augustine himself: "He must be understood to have said, 'I am not afraid to die because we have a good Master' lest it be thought that he had spoken what he said first: 'I have not lived in such a way that I am ashamed to stay alive among you,' confident of the purity of his own merits. He made this latter statement only as far as one man is able to understand another. He put more trust in God when it came to the examination of his goodness. Every day he asked God, 'Forgive us our debts.'"[12] This is how St. Augustine interpreted the great eloquence of the dying Ambrose. These other men, however, consoled themselves with their own merits.

I would like to know what a person can call his own except "his wrongdoing, which he recognizes, and his sin, which is always against him."[13] When he thinks of this sin, unless he has lost his senses, he exclaims, "Have mercy on me" to that One Who is all that is good in him. In this way only his evils are his own, or if he wants to share his attributes with someone else, whatever virtue there is in a mortal man belongs to God alone. This cannot belong, or be said to belong, to another because even exterior objects belong to God, although we concede to the common crowd that they may be said to belong to fortune.

The weak little body remains, and that too is a gift of God, but it sometimes is diseased, and death awaits it. What then is left except sin? Because it is voluntary and does not come from any other place than from the soul itself, it is clearly the only thing a human being can call his own. No one is such a slave of sin that he does not know that he can have no consolation or glory from what belongs to others, and in those things which he has in his own power there is much material for shame and fear.

I freely acknowledge Cicero's glory as long as I can, but because this is not now permitted, I willingly accept the defense of this great man, or rather I invent one for my own benefit. He was certainly a man of strong and sharp, agile and swift intellect (a praiseworthy quality in acting). How far, however, can speed take a man when he blocks his own way? God, Who gave him a quick intellect, closed off for him the access to Truth which He subsequently deemed worthy for us who are of slow intellect. Therefore, the swift intellect of Cicero and his comrades goes nowhere, but our ability, slow as it is, moves ever forward step by step, thanks to Him, to Whom the progress of our intellect and the levelness of our path are gifts. Nor am I doubtful that Cicero, if he only knew what we know, would say that man has no merit in himself, but Cicero was not strong enough to raise his sharp eyes to the very rays of truth, but, unless I am mistaken, he was worthy of having a better fate. I put it this way so that the excellence of his intellect might earn some grace. Maybe he would have done this if he had known Who had given him such an excellent intellect, but not knowing where to throw the anchor of his hope, he turned his prow onto the rocks of human presumption with the result that he mistakenly said that his departing life would find within itself solace for its misfortune.

Even if this were to excuse Cicero, where, pray tell, would those others find hope beyond themselves, whose gods deceived their worshipers while they were alive and deserted them when they were dead? I am not inventing some new false accusation against the gods of the Gentiles. The greatest of their poets put Juno to flight at the impending death of Turnus, whose life and victory she had favored.[14] Statius, who imitated Vergil in everything, depicted Apollo deserting his augur at Thebes at his death.[15] They are certainly false or fragile gods (or both, I would more likely believe), who abandon their followers in death when they are most in need of help. Our God, however, has deserted His followers neither in life nor in death, "and has descended with them into the pit and has not left them in chains."[16] It was with this hope that David consoled himself: "If I walk in the midst of the shadow of death, I will not fear evil because

You are with me."[17] Do not the gods of the Gentiles, who are all demons, usually desert their followers in death or at the point of extreme and hopeless misfortune? They already desert them when their problems are much less serious and at every change of fortune, as if they follow only the power and wealth of a winner rather than the merits of the defeated.

Thus at every age of men worship and faith, ever-changing with fortune, are attributed to the gods in such a way that whoever opens his eyes can easily see what sort of "god" would desert those who are miserable and flatter only those who are lucky. I speak of a matter which you may not have heard before, but is familiar and very well known to us. When utter disaster was on the threshold, it was the custom among our ancestors to call out the protecting gods of besieged cities by certain incantations and to transfer them into the conquering city, leaving the besieged city undefended. Troy is proof of this. The greatest of the poets said, "You see the ways of fortune: all the gods on whom this kingdom had stood have left their shrines and have abandoned their altars."[18] The city of Veii provides another example. The victorious Roman leader is said to have brought from there into the very city of Rome the worship of Juno, who was revered at Veii with the greatest religious devotion.[19] So many other cities provide the same testimony that they claim that this was the only reason why the true name of Rome was unknown, lest through some reversal of fortune the Romans might suffer what they had done to so many others. This, they say, is the meaning of the statue of Angerona, with her finger placed on her lips, beckoning a vow of silence.[20] They add that a plebeian tribune was sentenced to death because he had revealed this secret.

Our God, however, favors humanity's merits, not its fortune. He never deserts those states which are under His protection unless their own lack of faith and godliness provoke Him. On the contrary, all hope is in God, that of the besieged as well as of all who toil. This is what the Christian congregation sings: "If God shall not guard our state, in vain the man who guards it stays awake."[21] We must honor and worship this God Who is the best guide of our life and death. We must place no hope in ourselves, but all hope in Him. Therefore, so that I may bring this part of this work to a close, remember that death is truly met with the calmest mind when a dying life can find consolation, not in its own merits, which do not exist (if we want to face the truth), but with Another's merits, that is, those of its Creator, that is, with mercy, with hope of pardon, and with the memory of countless blessings. Let us hope and pray that this may happen to us, and let those others, in their vanity, keep their own hope, their own merits, their own virtues, and their own fortune in this life. Let us humbly await our own reward from Another.

🏵 🏵 🏵

NOTES

1. Horace, *Epistles* 1.18.111-12, but Horace says "Jupiter," not "god."
2. Horace, *Odes* 1.31.17-20.
3. 1 Cor. 4:7.
4. This is probably a marginal note of Petrarch, mistakenly incorporated into the text.
5. Augustine, *Of True Religion* 7.12.
6. Ibid.
7. Cicero, *Tusculan Disputations* 1.45.109.
8. Cicero, *Stoic Paradoxes* 2.18.
9. Ps. 33:3.
10. 1 Cor. 1:31.
11. Possidonius, *Life of Augustine* 27; Paulinus, *Life of Ambrose* 45.
12. Possidonius, *Life of Augustine* 27.
13. Ps. 50:5.
14. Vergil, *Aeneid* 12.841-42.
15. Statius, *Thebaid* 7.789-90.
16. Wisd. 10:13-14.
17. Ps. 22:4.
18. Vergil, *Aeneid* 2.350-52.
19. Livy, *From the Founding of the City* 5.21.3.
20. Pliny, *Natural History* 3.5[9].65. Angerona was an obscure Roman goddess usually depicted with her mouth bound up and sealed. She was worshipped on 21 December, which may connect her name with the Latin verb *angerere*, "to rise up," and the winter solstice. Cf. Macrobius, *Satires* 3.9.1-6.
21. Ps. 126:1.

7

My brothers, we have the final goal, a thing which the great minds of antiquity did not have, to which we should direct the course of our life. "The light has risen on those who live in the region of the shadow of death,"[1] and a path has been revealed to us in the darkness. "Therefore, let us walk while we have the light lest the darkness overtake us."[2] We are about to come to Him "Who inhabits the unapproachable light, in Whose light we will see the light."[3] Take time, therefore, see this, and as we find in another citation of the Psalms, "Taste and see that God is sweet."[4] By taking time you will see that He Himself is God. By tasting you will see how sweet He is. By taking time, indeed, one can see and taste His divine sweetness. To this sight and taste has been added endless pleasure. Consequently, the greatest good resides in free time and leisure.

Look even further at yourselves and be admonished by what they claim to be the ancient advice of Apollo: "Know thyself." In short, look at all mortal matters which are under heaven, look at yourselves with all the others, and look at the world itself, which some people idly think to be everlasting. See how in the end everything which was created from nothing is taken away by great force, and if they did not abide in Him Who created them, they would be reduced to nothing. Abide rather in Him to Whom alone this saying pertains: "I am Who I am."[5] For us the safe, pleasant, fortunate, and delightful thing to do is "to cling to the Good."[6]

He has created you from nothing and with His own blood has reformed you who have fallen to nothing as you drown in sin. We must beg Him to "protect us under the shadow of His own wings from the sight of the wicked people who have beset us,"[7] and cherishing us in His sacred embrace when we are exhausted by heavy labor, to take pity on us lest we slip back into nothingness. Because I have been actively arguing for religious leisure, I have developed this idea so that you may always take time from useless and aimless concerns, so that you may never take time away from those which are useful.

"The most important matters concern the safety of one's country," said Cicero.[8] I do not deny this, but, my brothers, because your love and desire for the eternal Jerusalem have taken you away from the concern for this earthly fatherland, your greatest concern is for the salvation of your soul. Your obligation to render divine praises to God requires a large part of your time. The needs of nature, which are all too difficult and cannot be denied, require only a part of your time.

Devote your remaining time to religious literature so the twisting serpent will not find its own kind among you nor any chink in the armor of your souls. Train your mind in these matters, my brothers. Keep your eyes, ears, and tongue focused on this. Concentrate on this alone. You can do nothing better, more productive, more pleasant, for this is that "dwelling place in the lands of the kingdom of heaven"[9] about which Jerome writes to Paulinus. Therefore, just as Jerome begged him, so I beg you, my brothers, "to live among these matters, to meditate on them, to know nothing else, and to seek nothing else."[10] Be not moved by the "simplicity" of sacred Scriptures and the "crudeness" of its words. As the same man says, "either through some error of the interpreters or on purpose these have been articulated in such a way that an educated person may understand the same sentence in one way, but an uneducated person in another."[11] Whatever quality the surface may be, there is nothing sweeter than the innermost part, nothing more delightful, nothing better for us.

Therefore, of all writings, this one is obviously the most noble, although the jealous may be consumed with envy, the proud may puff themselves up, and deaf ears may not hear the truth; each time we hear the general term "writings," we understand this writing alone, by means of that which the Greeks called metonymy.

Of course, what I am asserting now I would have denied not many years ago, in public or even to myself. I thank Him Who has opened my eyes so that I might see what I could not see clearly before. May He also clear my eyes, which are foggy, so that I may see what I still cannot see because of my damnable dullness. I am less disappointed in myself when I hear St. Jerome himself, who turned his attention to sacred writings only after being engrossed in the books of the Gentiles, confess that "their unrefined speech horrified him."[12] If this could happen to such a man who had been very well trained in sacred Scripture since adolescence, why could it not happen to me, a sinner whom I would not call learned in secular literature, lest I lie, but delighted by it, nevertheless, since my infancy? I have had as my teachers, not Gregory of Nazianzus, as he did, nor anyone else of high intelligence, or at least of a faithful and devoted mind, but rather I have had those who ridiculed as old wives' tales the Psalms of David, which contain more wisdom in a single page than any other writing whatsoever. With this sort of impression my tender and easily swayed mind was to be molded! What a great concern fathers ought to have for their sons, who are of such a malleable age, if they love their sons, as they should, and not themselves. More truly, if they love, not themselves, but the advantages to be derived from their sons. Thus unlucky boys are brought up for civil law, for skills which promote greed, and for purposeless eloquence. They look down on and abandon life-bringing Scriptures, and if anyone embraces the Scriptures, profit is the motive of their thoughts and hopes. In this way the divine grace of heavenly words has now been turned into the commerce of earthly goods.

But I return to myself. Late in my life, very late, and with no guide, I began to find the Truth. At first I had doubts, but then I began to move forward step by step, under the care of Him Who always knows how to use our misfortunes for His own glory, often for our own salvation. Although it would take a huge volume to list my vacillations and failings, it became clear to me in that confused process that I needed to read St. Augustine's *Confessions*. Why do I not confess about him what he confesses about Cicero?[13] St. Augustine first guided me to the love of Truth. He first taught me to live wholesomely after I had lived fruitlessly for so long. Let him rest blessed in eternity without end, whose hand first offered me that book which brought my wandering mind under control.[14] I have been delighted by the lofty and salutary genius of the man and by his eloquence, which is not too elaborate, but sober and serious, and by his complex, yet varied and efficacious teachings.

Why am I saying so much? I began to follow him, still timid, similar to someone embarrassed to change his purpose (which is common enough for those who feel pride). I set out with my old interests, reckless habits, and desperation for reform calling me back, for I feared losing what I had struggled to accumulate my whole life, however insignificant those possessions might have been. Nevertheless, I followed him, slowly at first, and devoted all my days to this purpose. Then I proceeded with a little more speed, and finally I progressed quickly, as if somehow I could, as Seneca says, "procure time with speed."[15] With God's help it turned out more successfully than I hoped, so it was by him that I was first snatched and gradually lured from my ways. St. Ambrose, who must be named with a bowed head, came to me. St. Jerome and St. Gregory followed next. Then St. John with his golden voice, and Lactantius, overflowing with his milky currents of nourishing words, also came to my aid. Thus, full of awe, with this very illustrious company, I entered the realm of sacred Scriptures, which I had previously scorned, and I found that everything was contrary to what I had thought. A therapeutic need brought me to praise God and my daily obligation to glorify Him, which I had wrongfully put off. For this reason, I have often been forced to reflect upon David's Psalms, a source from which I have been eager to drink, not that I might become a more learned man, but a better one, if I could, nor that I could come out of it a better dialectician, but a less corrupt sinner.

Therefore, as a stranger lured by their soothing balms, I fell in love with these still unknown Scriptures, albeit late in life. You, however, being native-born to them and nourished by them from the beginning, should love, cultivate, venerate, and pursue them frequently. Never let them fall from your hands, if that could be possible, and surely never let them fall from your thoughts.

If, however, you seek some authority for these Scriptures, they have been uttered by the Holy Ghost and confirmed by the voice of Christ. If you seek their antiquity, they come entirely before all secular writings — these writings were famous in the whole world before the birth of Cadmus, the founder of the Greeks, Isis of the Egyptians, and Carmentis, the ancestress of the Latins. If you seek virtue, "those arrows are sharp" and glowing which restore to life those hearts which they have pierced. If you seek profit, the fruit of other "arrows" is either a brief profit, transient glory, or false favor; the destination of these "arrows" is eternal life and true happiness. If you seek adornment, I can say many things about this, yet this is the most important point of all, that some things may perchance be more attractive on the surface, but nothing is truly more beautiful than the sacred Scriptures.

On one hand, I want you to imagine a beautiful woman, one who is sober, chaste, and content with simple dress; and on the other hand, a most exquisitely molded harlot, her face richly adorned with makeup. Is anyone so stupid that he doubts which one he would rather marry?

Many men have been great and educated, and some have been eloquent. It seems that it is easier to find an educated man than an eloquent one, but in fact, the reason is right before our eyes because learning is able to exist without eloquence, but eloquence cannot exist without learning. Eloquence has to be varied and complex, unless by chance we should prefer the loquacious person to one who is truly eloquent. Nothing is more deceptive than that, and this explains the rarity of poets and orators which Cicero discussed with such inspiration in his *Orator*.[16] Although it would take too long to count the total number who have flourished from the beginning of time up to this day in every part of the world, the whole cohort of wise and eloquent men all philosophize, dispute, orate, and embellish their subjects with whatever style they choose, dressing their subjects with the thinnest of artifices and poetic veils. Will they not all seem uneducated and ineloquent when Christ's voice thunders in opposition, and the supreme truth of that saying of the regal prophet David becomes clear? "Their judges have been swallowed up and bound with rock."[17] Swallowed up, I say, in reference to that rock, by which Christ is signified. At this point those who made themselves out to be the greatest all in themselves will be seen as absolutely nothing.

My brothers, this is everything I have chosen to write concerning religious leisure, although I am by no means ignorant that this discourse can be prolonged as long as suffering endures, of which we know there is no end. Nevertheless, I have spoken enough for now. I need to hear the rest from you, who from experience are masters in these matters. This leisure and free time will offer you the chance to see that God Himself is our Master. Knowledge of Him will help you to scrutinize those things which are most appropriate for your salvation, especially your flight from temporal problems. It will help you to reject resolutely the senses, so you will not be caught by the deceit of this world, the flesh, and demons, so you will not trust in enemies or evil counselors, and finally so that you will not be torn away weeping or unwilling from where one ought to be torn.

You have chosen a glorious and quiet place to see these things, you have taken a path which is straight and free from worries, and you have anointed your eyes with an effective balm. So come, continue in the direction in which you have begun.[18] Let nobody turn back. That salt statue of the woman looking backwards[19] has seasoned your souls with its healthy flavor. No one is without sin, but the sinner is told, "Have you sinned? Be quiet."[20] Therefore, be quiet, take time, make good use of your leisure, see, rejoice, weep for me, and fare well, ever mindful of me. O how fortunate you are if you know yourselves and your own blessings![21]

❧ ❧ ❧

NOTES

1. Isa. 9:2.
2. John 12:35.
3. 1 Tim. 6:16, Ps. 35:10.
4. Ps. 33:9.
5. Exod. 3:14.
6. Ps. 72:28.
7. Ps. 16:8-9.
8. Cicero, *On the State* 6.29.
9. Jerome, *Epistles* 53.9.
10. Ibid.
11. Ibid.
12. Jerome, *Epistles* 22.30.
13. Cf. Augustine, *Confessions* 3.4.
14. Dionysius of San Sepulcro gave Petrarch a copy of Augustine's *Confessions* in 1333.
15. Seneca, *Epistles* 68.13.
16. Cf. Cicero, *The Orator* 5.18, 20.
17. Ps. 140:6.
18. Cf. Apoc. 3.18; Cicero, *Against Catiline* 1.5.
19. Lot's wife was turned to a pillar of salt when she turned back to look at Sodom and Gomorrah, which they were fleeing. Cf. Gen. 19:26.
20. Cf. Ecclus. 21:1.
21. Cf. Vergil, *Georgics* 2.490.

BIBLIOGRAPHY

PUBLISHED VERSIONS OF THE TEXT

Opera Francisci Petrarchae. Basel: Johannes Amerbach, 1496.

Librorum Francisci Petrarchae Impressorum Annotatio. 2 vols. Venice: Andrea Torresani for Simone de Luere, 1501.

Librorum Francesci Petrarche Impressorum Annotatio. Venice: Simone Papiense, 1503.

Francisci Petrarchae...reflorescentis literaturae Latinaeque linguae...assertoris et instauratoris, opera quae extant omnia. 4 vols. Basel: Henricus Petri, 1554.

Francisci Petrarcha...Opera quae extant omnia. 4 vols. in 2. Basel: Sebastian Henricipetri, 1581.

De otio religiosorum. De vera sapientia. Berne: Iohannes Le Preux, 1604.

Francesci Petrarchae operum tomus primus.... Berne and Geneva: Pseudo edition of Iohannes Le Preux, 1610.

Il "De otio religioso" di Francesco Petrarca. Giuseppe Rotondi, ed. Studi e Testi 195. Vatican City: Biblioteca Apostolica Vaticana, 1958.

TRANSLATIONS OF THE TEXT

De otio religiosorum prima traduzione italiana. Luigi Volpicelli, ed. Rome, 1928.

"Un volgarizzamento inedito quattrocentesco del *De otio religioso.*" Giuseppe Rotondi, ed. *Studi petrarcheschi* 3 (1950): 47-96.

De otio religioso. P.G. Ricci, trans. In *Prose.* G. Martellotti, et al., eds. La letteratura italiana. Storia e testi 7. Milan & Naples: Riccardo Ricciardi, 1954, 594-603.

De otio religioso. In *Opere latine.* A. Bufano, with B. Aracri and C.K. Regiani, eds. Turin: UTET, 1975, 567-809.

Le repos religieux: 1346-1357. Jean-Luc Marion and Christophe Carraud, eds. Grenoble: J. Millon, 2000.

RELATED WORKS BY PETRARCH

The Ascent of Mont Ventoux. Hans Nachod, trans. In *The Renaissance Philosophy of Man.* Ernst Cassirer, Paul Oskar Kristeller, and John Herman

Randall, Jr., eds. Chicago & London: University of Chicago Press, 1948, 36-46.

De vita solitaria. Buch I. Kritische Textausgabe und Ideengeschichtlicher Kommentar. K.A.E. Enenkel, ed. Leiden & New York: E.J. Brill, 1990.

The Life of Solitude by Francis Petrarch. Jacob Zeitlin, trans. Urbana: University of Illinois Press, 1924; reprint, Westport, CT: Hyperion Press, 1978.

Petrarch at Vaucluse. Letters in Verse and Prose. Ernest Hatch Wilkins, trans. and ed. Chicago: University of Chicago Press, 1958.

Petrarch's "Bucolicum carmen." Thomas G. Bergin, ed. & trans. New Haven & London: Yale University Press, 1977.

Petrarch's Lyric Poems. The "Rime sparse" and Other Lyrics. Robert M. Durling, trans. & ed. Cambridge, MA & London: Harvard University Press, 1976.

Remedies for Fortune Fair and Foul. Conrad Rawski, trans. & ed. Bloomington: Indiana University Press, 1991.

SECONDARY WORKS

Boyer, Raymond. *La Chartreuse de Montrieux aux XIIe et XIIIe siècles.* 2 vols. Marseilles: J. Laffitte, 1980.

Cochin, Henri. *Le frère de Pétrarque et le Livre du Repos des Religieux.* Paris: E. Bouillon, 1902.

Foresti, Arnaldo. "Quando Gherardo si fece monaco." *Aneddoti della vita di Francesco Petrarca: Nuova edizione corretta e ampliata dall'autore.* Studi sul Petrarca 1. Padua: Antenore, 1977, 108-14.

—. "Un saluto e un sospiro alla Certosa di Montrieux." Op. cit., 194-203.

Foster, Kenelm. *Petrarch: Poet and Humanist.* Writers of Italy 9. Edinburgh: Edinburgh University Press, 1984.

Kristeller, Paul Oskar. *Renaissance Thought: The Classic, Scholastic, and Humanist Strains.* New York: Harper & Row, 1961.

Leclercq, Jean. *"Otia monastica:* Étude sur le vocabulaire de la contemplation au moyen âge," *Studia Anselmiana* 51 (Rome, 1963): 27-41.

Mann, Nicholas. *Petrarch.* Past Masters Series. New York: Oxford University Press, 1984.

Mazzotta, Giuseppe. *The Worlds of Petrarch.* Duke Monographs in Medieval and Renaissance Studes 14. Durham, NC: Duke University Press, 1994.

Rotondi, Giuseppe. "Le due redazioni del *De otio* del Petrarca." *Aevum* 9 (1935): 27-77.

—. "Note al *De otio religioso.*" *Studi petrarcheschi* 2 (1949): 153-66.

Sieben, H.J. "'Quies' et 'Otium.'" In *Dictionnaire de spiritualité ascétique et mystique, doctrine et histoire* 12. Paris: Beauchesne, 1985, 2746-56.

Trinkaus, Charles. *"In Our Image and Likeness": Humanity and Divinity in Italian Humanist Thought.* 2 vols. London: Constable, 1970. Rpt. 1995.

Voci, Anna Maria. *Petrarca e la vita religiosa: Il mito umanista della vita eremitica.* Studi di storia moderna e contemporanea 13. Roma : Istituto storico italiano per l'età moderna e contemporanea, 1983.

Wilkins, Ernest Hatch. *Life of Petrarch.* Chicago & London: University of Chicago Press, 1961.

Witt, Ronald. *Hercules at the Crossroads: The Life, Writing, and Thought of Coluccio Salutati.* Durham, NC: Duke University Press, 1983.

—. *"In the Footsteps of the Ancients": The Origins of Humanism from Lovato to Bruni.* Leiden & Boston: E.J. Brill, 2000.

❧ ❧ ❧

INDEX OF CITATIONS

GENERAL INDEX

See also Index of Citations

This Book Was Completed on June 25, 2002
at Italica Press, New York, New York
and Was Set in Adobe Garamond.
It Was Printed on 60-lb. Natural
Paper by BookMobile,
St. Paul, MN
U.S.A.
🌿 🌿
🌿